CP L2
1124

Studying Comics
and Graphic Novels

S

Studying Comics and Graphic Novels

Karin Kukkonen

WILEY Blackwell

This edition first published 2013
© 2013 John Wiley & Sons, Ltd

Registered Office
John Wiley & Sons, Ltd, The Atrium, Southern Gate, Chichester, West Sussex, PO19 8SQ, UK

Editorial Offices
350 Main Street, Malden, MA 02148-5020, USA
9600 Garsington Road, Oxford, OX4 2DQ, UK
The Atrium, Southern Gate, Chichester, West Sussex, PO19 8SQ, UK

For details of our global editorial offices, for customer services, and for information about
how to apply for permission to reuse the copyright material in this book please see our website
at www.wiley.com/wiley-blackwell.

The right of Karin Kukkonen to be identified as the author of this work has been asserted in
accordance with the UK Copyright, Designs and Patents Act 1988.

Library of Congress Cataloging-in-Publication Data

Kukkonen, Karin, 1980–
  Studying comics and graphic novels / Karin Kukkonen.
    pages   cm
  Includes index.
    ISBN 978-1-118-49993-1 (cloth) – ISBN 978-1-118-49992-4 (pbk.)   1. Comic books,
strips, etc.–History and criticism.   2. Graphic novels–History and criticism.   I. Title.
  PN6710.K84 2014
  741.5′9–dc23

                                              2013015566
A catalogue record for this book is available from the British Library.

Cover image © Pavel Tretera / Shuttlestock
Cover design by Design Delux

Set in 10/13pt Minion by SPi Publisher Services, Pondicherry, India
Printed in Singapore by Ho Printing Singapore Pte Ltd

Contents

Acknowledgments   vii

Introduction: How to Use This Book   1
  What This Book Holds   2
  Working Definitions   4

1   What's in a Page: Close-Reading Comics   7

  Cognitive Processes and Critical Terms   7
  Navigating the Comics Page   16
  Entering the Storyworld and Meeting its Participants   19
  Comics Analysis – A Basic Checklist   26

2   The Way Comics Tell it: Narration and Narrators   31

  Showing and Telling   31
  Story, Discourse, and Plot   34
  The Narrator   39
  Narration, Focalization, and Point of View   44
  Narrative as Meaning-Making   48
  Graphic Narrative – A Basic Checklist   49

3   Narrating Minds and Bodies: Autobiographical Comics   55

  Style and Subjectivity   55
  Autographic Agents   57
  Embodiment   60
  Self-Reflexivity   61
  Time, Story, and History   65
  Alternative Agendas and Authenticity   68

4   Novels and Graphic Novels: Adaptations   73

    Transporting Stories   74
    Media Affordances and Adaptation Strategies   75
    Fidelity in Adaptation   80
    Literary Complexity   85
    The Page Revisited   90

5   Comics and Their History   99

    The Beginnings of Comics History   99
    Precursors in Emergent Mass Culture   102
    Newspaper Comics (1900s–1930s)   103
    The Comic Book (1930–54)   106
    Comics Censorship (1954)   110
    Comics as Popular Culture   113
    Breaking the Code 1: Pop Art and Underground Comix   117
    Breaking the Code 2: The British Invasion   118

6   The Study and Criticism of Comics   123

    Resources for Studying Comics   123
        Access to Comics Texts   123
        Critical Work on Comics   124
    Critical Approaches to Comics   125
        Comics Semiotics   126
        Comics Narratology   128
        Cognitive Approaches to Comics   129
        Historical and Auteurist Approaches   131
        Cultural Studies and Gender Studies   133
        Psychoanalysis   134
    How to Write Your Essay on Comics   139
        The Crime Scene   142
        The Witnesses   142
        Making Your Case   144
        End Credits   146

Conclusion: Comics as Literature   149
Appendix: More Comics and Graphic Novels to Read   155
Glossary   167
Index   179

Acknowledgments

Studying Comics and Graphic Novels has been a long-term project and learning process for me. First of all, my gratitude goes to my students at the Johannes Gutenberg-University Mainz (Germany) and Tampere University (Finland) who shared their enthusiasm, thoughts and comics knowledge with me. The comments of friends and colleagues on these chapters have improved the book beyond what I could have done on my own. In particular, I would like to thank those who read through different parts of the book in its final state: Ann Miller, Marco Caracciolo, Terence Cave, Jared Gardner, Laurence Grove, Sabine Müller, Roger Sabin and Emily Troscianko, as well as the publisher's anonymous readers. Whatever flaws remain are my own.

The Balzan Interdisciplinary Seminar "Literature as an Object of Knowledge" at St. John's College, Oxford, has been a supportive and inspiring environment for bringing this book to its conclusion. I gratefully acknowledge the financial support of the Balzan Seminar and of the English Department of the University of Oxford, and I sincerely thank the copyright holders who gave me permission to reproduce their images on these pages. Finally, my gratitude goes to Emma Bennett who believed in the project from the start and to Wiley Blackwell who saw the volume through production.

DC materials appear courtesy of DC Comics: *Desolation Jones* © Warren Ellis and J.H. Williams III. Used with Permission of DC Comics; *V for Vendetta*. © DC Comics. Used with Permission; *Sandman Vol.1: Preludes and Nocturnes*. © DC Comics. Used with Permission; From *Sandman Vol. 6: Fables and Reflections*. © DC Comics. Used with Permission; *Watchmen* © DC Comics. Used with Permission; *Promethea, Book 3* © DC Comics. Used with Permission.

Sinfest © 2012 Tatsuya Ishida. Laocoön. Source: Marie-Lan Nguyen, http://en.wikipedia.org/wiki/File:Laocoon_Pio-Clementino_Inv1059-1064-1067.jpg

Introduction: How to Use This Book

This book is a basic introduction to the study of COMICS and GRAPHIC NOVELS. It is designed to provide you with all the knowledge you need for studying and analyzing comics on a university course. It explores key issues in comics studies: how the MEDIUM tells its stories, how authors express their experience through them, what novels and graphic novels have in common and where they differ, as well as the history of comics as POPULAR CULTURE. The book outlines different critical approaches to comics, and gives you reading suggestions and exercises to practice comics analysis at the end of each chapter.

This book is for you, the reader of comics. It suggests an explanation for how we read comics and their NARRATIVES, how we relate to authors and NARRATORS and, perhaps, gives you a sense of how comics engage your mind. You might read this book in a class on comics and be interested in the reading suggestions and the exercises, or the instructions on how to write an essay on comics analysis; or you might be simply curious about what other people have to say and write about comics and graphic novels. Welcome. This section gives an overview of what you might expect in *Studying Comics and Graphic Novels* and sets out some basic definitions, but please feel free to skip ahead to any other chapter.

This book approaches comics through the ways in which they engage their readers' minds and bodies, and the processes through which readers make sense of the squiggles and lines on the page. These basic processes are the key this book offers for analyzing comics and for connecting close readings to larger issues, such as authenticity in autobiographic comics, media differences in comics ADAPTATIONS, or cultural evaluations of comics. *Studying Comics and Graphic Novels* is therefore based on a cognitive approach to comics, one

Studying Comics and Graphic Novels, First Edition. Karin Kukkonen.
© 2013 John Wiley & Sons, Ltd. Published 2013 by John Wiley & Sons, Ltd.

that draws on insights from the cognitive sciences and the neurosciences into how our minds and bodies work together. It uses the cognitive approach as a point of departure for considering different aspects of comics, their connection to other media, and their place in culture, but it will also introduce other approaches, from narratology to media studies and cultural studies on its journey. Concepts and terminology from these approaches will be introduced where needed.

What This Book Holds

Studying Comics and Graphic Novels has six chapters which address different thematic issues. The chapters are designed to build onto each other and to be read in sequence, leading from simple PANEL-by-panel analysis to a consideration of larger narrative strategies, and from the role of such formal and narrative strategies in autobiographic comics and comics adaptations to the place of comics in our cultural landscape. The chapters cross-reference each other, and if you prefer to read up on, say, Jane Austen adaptations before *Maus*, you will find pointers in each chapter that lead you back to previous discussions of particular terms and issues. The glossary similarly provides a ready set of definitions and explanations that will help you map your own path through this volume. Glossary entries are highlighted when they first appear in the text.

Chapter 1 What's In A Page outlines the basic elements of the comics page and the ways in which we read them. It introduces a set of critical terms for the basic elements of the comics page (like panel, GUTTER, MISE EN PAGE, etc.) and explains how they work together as CLUES from which readers draw INFERENCES as they make sense of what they see on a page. This chapter is designed to help you develop your skills for close readings of individual comics pages. It uses COMIC STRIPS and pages from a variety of WEB COMICS and printed comics.

Chapter 2 The Way Comics Tell It introduces you to storytelling in comics. It looks at the distinction between the text as it presents itself (in image, word, and sequence), the STORY we read from it, and the dynamics between story and DISCOURSE. In storytelling, there is always a teller, someone who relates the story, and this chapter outlines the different ways in which comics render narrators, perspective, and point of view in their narratives. It teaches you to identify and analyze the dynamics of storytelling and the strategies of storytellers in comics. It uses *The Sandman* as its core text.

Chapter 3 Narrating Minds and Bodies takes a closer look at the GENRE of autobiographical comics. It introduces the ways in which comics authors mark narratives as "theirs," as expressing their personal experience, and the narrative strategies which emerge from this, in terms of perspectives and EMBODI-MENT. Autobiographical comics aim for authenticity, and in this endeavor they often problematize the act of storytelling itself and the situation from which they tell their tale. This chapter specifies the narrative strategies of autobiographical comics, their self-reflexivity, and their relation to history. It also gives a brief overview of how the genre developed. Alison Bechdel's *Fun Home*, Craig Thompson's *Blankets*, and Art Spiegelman's *Maus* will serve as the basic texts.

Chapter 4 Novels and Graphic Novels addresses the adaptation of novels in comics. It outlines the basic media differences between novels and comics, and their respective capabilities in representing particular elements of a narrative. The questions of what it means to be "true" to the original text, and whether this is a goal to strive for, are discussed as well. This chapter compares the narrative strategies of the novel and comics and explains how comics adaptations can translate one medium into the other. It is designed to help you see the similarities in a comics and a novel version of the same text, and to discuss the relevant differences. Comics adaptations of Emily Brontë's *Wuthering Heights*, Jane Austen's *Sense and Sensibility*, and Laurence Sterne's *Tristram Shandy* will be used as example cases.

Chapter 5 Comics and Their History presents an overview of the history of comics in English-speaking countries, in particular the United States. This overview outlines the times and contexts in which comics have been produced, and the hierarchy of high culture and popular culture they are a part of. It regards comics as an instance of popular culture which has undergone a considerable reevaluation toward the end of the twentieth century. This chapter helps you gain a broader perspective on comics, and directs you to appreciate cultural and historical connections beyond the individual text. *Watchmen* is the suggested text for this chapter.

Chapter 6 The Study and Criticism of Comics introduces you to the research resources available on comics and to critical work on comics in different academic disciplines. An outline of how to get access both to comics texts, contemporary and historical, and to critical writing, is followed by a guided tour of six approaches to comics: semiotics, narratology, cognitive approaches, history, cultural studies and gender studies, and psychoanalysis. Each of the sections outlines the basic tenets of these approaches and explains which questions about comics they raise and help you answer. This chapter is designed to prepare you for writing your own research essay on comics. Installments from Winsor McCay's *Little Nemo in Slumberland* serve as examples through which the different approaches are put to work.

Each of the chapters features a number of text boxes which introduce a particular topic in more depth. In the chapter on comics adaptations, for example, the text boxes look at the *Classics Illustrated* series (which pioneered comics adaptations of "classic" novels), the graphic novel (and what meanings the term has in the context of publishing formats as opposed to the larger cultural debate), and the notion of convergence culture (according to which much of popular storytelling today emerges from an intermedial web). The text boxes are designed to give you more information on a particular issue raised in the main text, to connect this issue with more general questions, and to develop your critical vocabulary.

Apart from the text boxes, each chapter has recommended reading (with brief explanations of what the books suggested are about). The recommended reading lets you go on from the rather brief outlines this book provides to explore the issues yourself in greater depth. Each of the chapters also features a class activity, a writing exercise to practice comics analysis, and an essay topic connected to the topic of the chapter and the example texts discussed. At the end of the book, you will find a glossary explaining the critical terms introduced in the book and a list of more comics you might want to read.

Working Definitions

Before we get started, however, I should lay out the basic assumptions on which this book is built.

What are comics to begin with? Any number of scholars working on comics will give you any number of answers to this question. The basic definition of comics I work with here is that comics are a medium that communicates through images, words, and sequence. A medium is constituted in three ways: (i) it is a MODE of communication, (ii) it relies on a particular set of technologies, and (iii) it is anchored in society through a number of institutions (Jensen 2008). Comics work as a mode of communication in that they tell stories or present jokes in a particular manner using images, words, and sequence. Comics also rely on the technology of print and the format of the book. With the increasing digitalization of comics and the rise of web comics, a new set of technologies might be introduced for comics, but as of now, most comics are printed and bound in various formats. Comics are institutionalized; in the United States for example through the MAINSTREAM COMICS publishing houses, such as DC and Marvel. Independent and ALTERNATIVE COMICS, when they are self-published or (re)published and distributed through smaller publishers of comics, are tied to institutional infrastructures particular to comics as well. In this book, we will mostly focus on comics as a mode of communication, but the other two dimensions (technology and institutions) will come to the fore every now and then, particularly in the chapter on comics history.

Comics can be thought of as a "visual language" rather than as a medium, as for example Neil Cohn (2007) proposes. Their image sequences link instances of the visual into meaningful utterances, just like sentences arrange words into meaningful statements. Seeing comics as a visual language would imply that they are not tied to a particular technology or a particular set of institutions. Web comics, for example, feature a different set of technologies, because they are distributed digitally, other than COMIC BOOKS and graphic novels. Still, of course, they are perceived in the cultural framework of the comics medium, and the web comic I discuss in the first chapter of this book, *Sinfest*, is published in black-and-white strips on weekdays and colored pages on Sundays, just like the traditional newspaper comics. The technology and institution of the newspaper comics have shaped the way in which this web comic works. I have refrained from presenting comics as a "visual language" as opposed to a medium here, because the contexts within which comics are produced and read are highly important for the ways in which we understand them and make sense of them.

Images, words, and sequence are the three constituents of comics as a mode of communication. A panel usually holds an image as well as written words in CAPTIONS, SPEECH BUBBLES, or as sound effects (onomatopoeia), and several panels are arranged in sequence on a page. We will discuss these three constituents and the way they work in more detail in the next chapter. Here, I want to discuss briefly whether each of the constituents is necessary, a debate which scholars of comics have had for several decades now. Do we need images? After all, the speech bubble is perhaps the most iconic element of the comics form, and comics which use just speech bubbles are possible. Do we need words? Silent panels are not uncommon, even in mainstream comics, and there is an entire genre, called "SANS PAROLES," which can be described as comics without words. Do we need sequence? Or does an individual panel already constitute a comic? Perhaps we do not need each constituent in each instance of a comic, but all three serve as the basic elements through which what we call "comics" unfolds.

Involving the different constituents of images, words, and sequence, comics are often created by more than one person. *Watchmen*, for example, was written by Alan Moore, penciled and inked by Dave Gibbons and colored by Alan Higgins. When we therefore talk of "Alan Moore's *Watchmen*," we ignore the (significant) contributions of the two other creators of the comics. Of course, there are also many examples of comics in which one author writes, illustrates, colors and letters the entire narrative, such as Winsor McCay or Will Eisner, and most importantly, the autobiographical comics. In this book, I will therefore talk of Winsor McCay's *Little Nemo in Slumberland,* because McCay is the single author, but will simply talk of *The Sandman,* because besides Neil Gaiman, who is the writer of the series, there are about forty other creators involved. In the list of comics and graphic novels at the end of this book, you will find the fuller (if not always complete) credits for each of the comics discussed here.

By now, you should have an idea of what this book is about, the issues it raises in the individual chapters, and what the working definitions are. It has probably also become clear what this book does not do. Even though the basic accounts of close reading comics and comics storytelling in Chapters 1 and 2 are partly built on research in French-language comics and should be useful for reading BANDE DESSINÉE and MANGA as well, *Studying Comics* focuses on English-language comics and leaves aside other great comics traditions, such as France and Belgium as well as Japan. Even though I discuss some web comics, my history of comics ends at the turn of the twenty-first century. These limitations are partially due to the ignorance of the author (particularly in the case of manga), and partially due to the endeavor to keep this volume as coherent and concise as possible. After all, it is an introduction.

Recommended Reading

Hatfield, Charles. 2005. *Alternative Comics: An Emerging Literature.* Jackson: University of Mississippi Press. Chapter 2: The Otherness of Comics Reading.

References

Cohn, Neil. 2007. "The Visual Language Manifesto: Restructuring the 'Comics' Industry and Its Ideology." Accessed October 15, 2012. Emaki.net/manifesto. html

Jensen, Klaus Bruhn. 2008. "Media." *International Encyclopedia of Communication,* ed. Wolfgang Donsbach. Oxford: Wiley-Blackwell.

1

What's in a Page: Close-Reading Comics

Comics seem more straightforward than written texts. Because they have images, it appears that everyone understands immediately what is going on their pages. However, as you begin to seriously consider comics and the way they tell their story, you will realize that also analyzing comics is a skill that has to be practiced. Close-reading comics is the first stepping stone toward understanding how they unfold their meaning. This chapter will explain how reading comics works by relating the elements of the comics page to what is going on in your mind as you make sense of them. It also introduces the basic terms you will need for your own comics' analysis.

Cognitive Processes and Critical Terms

The comic strip from the web comics series *Sinfest* you will find on the next page seems immediately accessible: it presents a short dialogue between a boy and a girl. The girl seems to be in control of the situation, dispensing advice to the boy, until he turns the situation around in the final panel as he challenges her moral superiority. Yet this account short-circuits your encounter with this comic: when you read a panel like the first one, your mind begins taking in all kinds of information from the images and the written text – the facial expressions, gestures, and postures of the CHARACTERS, their speech, the layout of the image and many other features. These are clues for you to make sense of the panel and the event it represents. You identify clues, you draw inferences from them, and you integrate these inferences into the basic pattern of the story. These processes are not conscious proceedings, but something which you do (almost automatically).

Studying Comics and Graphic Novels, First Edition. Karin Kukkonen.
© 2013 John Wiley & Sons, Ltd. Published 2013 by John Wiley & Sons, Ltd.

Figure 1.1   *Sinfest* (I). Source: Sinfest: Viva La Resistance™ © 2012 Tatsuya Ishida.

If you want to analyze comics critically, it makes sense to consider how the clues on the page and the inferences they suggest tie in with how you make sense of the comic. The cognitive processes involved in reading comics are usually pre-conscious, that is, you would not be aware of them when you are actually reading a comic, but they contribute fundamentally to your meaning-making.

First, however, in order to make the analysis as specific as possible, I will briefly introduce some basic terminology for the comic and its elements. The *Sinfest* comic is structured into four panels which are the boxes within which you see the characters. Each panel presents something like a snapshot of the action, relating to what has happened before and suggesting how the event might continue. Within the panels, you see the characters and you can read their communication in the SPEECH BUBBLES. Speech bubbles are spaces within which the characters' words are rendered in written text. The tail of the speech bubble is connected to the mouth of the speaker, allowing you to relate the written text to its speaker. When the speech is not located with a speaker in the image, it is rendered in a caption, a box usually at the top left-hand corner of the panel.

As you make your way through a panel, your might first get a (very rough) impression of the entire panel. This is an impression of the number of characters and their general spatial relation to each other, as well as the number of speech bubbles and their connection to the characters. This is the snapshot aspect of the panels. In the first panel, for example, you can see at first glance that the girl is in control. She is the only one speaking, privileged by her position in the left-to-right reading direction of the panel, and she points at the boy, defining him. The boy, on the other hand, stands, with his hands in his pockets, which signals being relaxed. Without even reading the speech bubbles, we can tell that this power relationship will change in the final panel, because here the image shows us the protagonists from the other side of the encounter (which looks like the image has been flipped around), and the girl's body suddenly tenses up. This information on basic power relationships and attitudes is something you can take in at a single glance, because they relate to your own bodily experience of the world. Try sitting up in your chair, and you will feel more alert; put your hands in your pockets and slump back, and you will be more relaxed.

When we see characters do something in a panel, the processes in our brains unfold something like an imitation of these postures in motorsensory systems which prepare the action (but do not lead us to actually perform it), and we feel an echo of the character's experience. This has been discussed in terms of "embodied simulation" in the neurosciences. When an image relates characters to each other in its COMPOSITION, our BODY SCHEMA (that is, our motorsensory capacities, see Gallagher 2005) give us a sense of whether there is a balance or an imbalance between the characters, and how the dynamics of the relationship is going to unfold. In his discussion of the dynamics of composition in art, Rudolf Arnheim (2008) has noted how perception and our bodily experience of balance, gravity and other forces shape each other. What the cognitive sciences have found about the relation of body and mind suggests that a good part of our meaning-making is indeed grounded in our bodily experience of the world. A lot of information can be taken in at a single glance.

As you investigate the details of the panel then, your attention focuses and you read the speech bubbles. When you pay attention to the details of the panel, it begins to unfold through time, and a story emerges as you relate the first-glance information to the details you pick up now. The controlling attitude of the girl is confirmed, when we read that she indeed tells the boy "what you gotta do." His smart tie and carefully groomed hair suggest that he thinks highly enough of himself to take care of his appearance. The sunglasses also contribute to this attitude of studied coolness. The clothes and the looks of characters give you a lot of information, based on social conventions and expectations, about the way they want to be perceived and about what is important to them.

The girl's speech is modulated by her gestures (pointing at the boy, calling him to attention, and referring to herself) and her facial expressions of emotional states. It is also shaped by the emphasis of the letters in bold, which indicate stress in her voice. In her final word, "diva," she seems to be positively yelling. Unlike the printed letters on a book page, the letters in speech bubbles have onomatopoetic qualities, which means that their size and boldness correspond to the volume at which they are spoken and the emphasis which is laid onto them. The bigger and bolder the letters, the louder the speech; the smaller and thinner the letters, the more quiet and subdued.

Paying attention to the details on the page fleshes out the basic impression that you get from the first glance. Your inferences get more precise and you get a clearer sense of what the story is about, of the interests and investments of the characters involved, and also of the likely course the action is going to take. The scene between the girl and the boy is set up as an encounter between two different attitudes: know-it-all versus studied cool. This is information which you can take from their body language, but also from the social knowledge you have about clothing style for example. In the beginning it looks like the girl has all the trumps in her hand: she is the only one speaking and shaping the space of interaction between them with her gestures (thereby assigning him a particular role in the encounter). Readers not only infer the meaning of the situation as it stands, but also project how the story will continue on the basis of their inferences: Will the boy accept the girl's assessment of his tuition? Will he try to turn the situation around? Will he lose his cool? These are all questions raised by the first panel. As the following panels give answers to these questions and raise new ones, your inferences about the situation, the relations of the characters and the potential outcome will change constantly, and a narrative emerges as you establish connections between the events.

In this particular comic, the panel images represent a single situation, set in a single space, and the dialogue unfolds continuously. Other comics, however, might feature long temporal gaps between panels or they might change scenes completely between panels. The space between the panels is called the "gutter", and just as you step across a gutter, your mind creates connections between the individual panels, by drawing inferences about how the action in the one can relate to the other, and thereby trying to integrate them into a single, meaningful narrative.

Scott McCloud calls the phenomenon of making sense between panels "closure" (1994, 67). To McCloud, who has a very broad-ranging understanding of closure, it is a process that turns readers into participants of the comics' narrative as they supply the missing information between panels. Closure goes back to the so-called "principle of closure" in GESTALT psychology. We perceive the Figure 1.2 as a

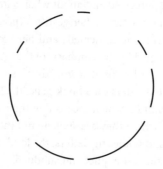

Figure 1.2　Closure.

circle, even though it is in fact an assortment of curved lines. We close the visual gaps and see a complete shape rather than lines. However, this does not mean that we have a very precise sense of the lines that fill the gaps. We simply assume that they most likely continue in roughly the same color, thickness, and curvature that we observe in the parts of the circle that we do see. Once the principle of closure is moved to panel-to-panel transitions, there is the tacit assumption that we have the same characters and locations at a slightly later point in time but we do not run an inner film of how they got there.

Consider the bodily forces of composition at work in the first row of panels in Figure 1.3. The composition of the two bodies describes a half-arc, and the impetus of the movement is from left to right. The movement of Charlotte's mother determines Charlotte's motion here, and it directs your attention. Like a wrestler, she seems to fling her daughter's body along the left to right arc. Once we have a closer look at the background of the second and third panel, however, we notice that the movement is not continuous. The mother's body has not just turned (which would be the easiest way for joining up the circle), but she has actually changed her position in the room.

The whole, the circle, we perceive, reflects the "mental model" we construct as we make sense of a narrative. We construct a mental model of the characters,

Figure 1.3   Bad Machinery. © John Allison.

the relations between them and the events that affect them. This mental model is the basis for the STORYWORLD, which we will discuss in the final section of this chapter (see Herman 2002). In some cases, such as the *Sinfest* and the *Bad Machinery* comics, this mental model is rather simple and straightforward. In other cases, developing a coherent mental model and a narrative out of your inferences presents much more of a challenge.

What is a narrative in the first place? "The cat sat on the mat" is no narrative because nothing is happening. "The cat sat on the dog's mat," however, has the potential for a conflict and for a chain of actions to unfold, and it therefore constitutes a minimal narrative, as Gerald Prince (1982, 147) suggests. In the first instance, we can say that a narrative is a chain of events that sets up a conflict and that keeps us wondering about what will happen next. I will elaborate this account in the next chapter. For now, back to *Sinfest*.

The narrative movement of the encounter in Figure 1.4 is reflected in the composition of the comic as a whole. There are alternating changes between the perspective of the panels: panel 1 shows the little devil watching TV; in panel 2, when the TV set unexpectedly begins to interact with the devil, we have a similar jump across the axis of the gaze between TV and devil as in the final panel of Figure 1.1; panel 3 shows a view from being the devil; panel 4 reestablishes the perspective of the first panel. This reflects the ways in which the TV set gains ascendance over the devil. From an unobtrusive position in the right-hand corner of the panel, the TV set literally "jumps" into prominence (and the left-hand corner) in the second panel. It towers above the little devil in the perspective of the third panel until it moves back into

Figure 1.4   *Sinfest* (II) Source: Sinfest: Viva La Resistance™© 2012 Tatsuya Ishida.

the unobtrusive position of the forth panel. Through the arrangement of perspectives in the panels, the TV set seems to circle around the little devil, asserting its dominance from every angle. The changes of perspective between panels, and the movements of bodies across a strip or a page are often used to underline narrative developments.

Another way to work out what is going on within and between panels are the gazes of the characters. If characters look at something, chances are it's important. The gaze of the little devil is almost glued to the TV set, stressing its hypnotizing presence. Charlotte in Figure 1.3 keeps her eyes closed in the first two panels to avoid engaging with her surroundings, and her mother's dramatically averted gaze suggests that she would rather not be part of this encounter either. In the *Sinfest* comic, the fixed gaze of the little devil keeps redirecting readers to the TV set. Gazes guide our attention as we read

Box 1.1   *Lessing and Laocoön*

Figure 1.5   Laocoön. Source: Wikimedia Commons. Marie-Lan Nguyen, http://en.wikipedia.org/wiki/File:Laocoon_Pio-Clementino_Inv1059-1064-1067.jpg

In 1766, the German critic Gotthold Ephraim Lessing wrote a treatise called "Laocoön: An Essay on the Limits of Painting and Poetry." More than a century before the emergence of comics as a medium, Lessing's essay outlined a key critical issue which occupies comics scholars still today: what words and images can and cannot do. Lessing takes his cue from the famous statue of Laocoön (Figure 1.5). Laocoön was a priest who predicted the fall of Troy and was silenced by the gods. The statue shows the moment in which Laocoön and his sons are attacked and killed by sea-snakes. In the *Aeneid*, in which Virgil retells the event in words, readers get the full story. Lessing now distinguishes between painting as an "art of space" and poetry as an "art of time." The statue of Laocoön unfolds in space through the bodies it depicts; Virgil's epic poem unfolds in time as you read it through line by line. Lessing carves out different aesthetic territories for images and words, relating each to different parameters of our experience of the world (time and space).

Lessing's account would suggest that comics are a mixed medium which unduly confuses basic aesthetic categories. However, if you take a close look at the statue of Laocoön, this distinction between time and space starts to get a bit blurry. As you engage with the statue, you look at the different details of it (the facial expressions, the snakes ready to strike, etc.) and then it *does* unfold in time. As you read a poem, you read the block of text as the words relate back and forth across the page, and then it *does* unfold in space. Lessing himself admits that poetry can gesture towards space and bodies, and that painting can gesture towards time and actions. Indeed, rather than confusing what words and images can do, it seems that comics are a medium which capitalizes on the overlaps of these AFFORDANCES. The words attain a spatial quality, as they are couched in speech bubbles that are located in relation to characters. The images in the panels attain a temporal quality, as you read their details bit by bit and as they are presented in sequence. Lessing's distinction works as a helpful tool for thinking through the ways in which the spatial and temporal qualities inter-mesh in comics.

With the "PREGNANT MOMENT," Lessing introduces another concept which we will keep coming back to in this book.[1] Images represent the "pregnant moment" of an action, the moment which captures the crucial point about a situation. It allows you to infer what happened in the past, and it lets you project what will happen in the future. Even if we can take in much information in a single glance, as we saw for the first *Sinfest* comic, each of the panels also implies a temporal extension. In the *Bad Machinery* comic, Charlotte is eating, but this cannot happen at the same time as her talking to her mother, because it's rather hard to articulate when you have a spoon in your mouth. There is a double time scheme at work in this panel: the girl is finally, and defiantly, having her breakfast, and the spoon in her mouth communicates this at a single glance. What she says in her speech bubble, on the other hand, gives the panel and her attitude its extension in time. Reading though the text in the speech bubble and paying attention to the details of the images allow you to connect the "pregnant moment" with the larger continuity of what happened before and what happened afterwards.

Box 1.2   *Faces, Emotions, and Characters*

The faces of comics characters are spaces which give you textual clues as dense as any speech bubble. You can draw inferences on the basis not only of gaze patterns (as discussed above), but also on the basis of their facial features and expressions. The facial features of a character are often stereotyped, that is formed according to cultural prejudices, and give you information on what kind of character you are dealing with. Physiognomy, the art of assessing personality from facial features, has been discounted as unscientific by contemporary psychology. However, comics use stereotypical features to allow readers to make snap judgments about characters. Rodolphe Töpffer, one of the founding fathers of comics, wrote a treatise called "Essay on Physiognomy" (1845), in which he outlines how minute changes of facial features create a completely different impression of personality.

Facial expressions, on the other hand, give you an idea of what a character feels. If they are sad, angry, or thoughtful, these emotions will be communicated through the look on their faces. The girl's expression in the fourth panel of the *Sinfest* comic tells you a lot about what she is feeling. Her eyes widen in anger, and her body language communicates mounting tenseness as she gets angry. The facial expression of the girl, in contrast to her aloof superiority before, gives the final panel its punch. Facial expressions, bodily postures that go with them, communicate the mental states of characters to us, and this is a line of inquiry still pursued by psychology today.

The psychologist Paul Ekman distinguishes between six basic facial expressions, which connote anger, disgust, fear, happiness, sadness and surprise, and can (to some extent) be understood across cultures. In comics, these facial expressions never stand on their own but are always embedded in a narrative context which helps you specify them. Emotions can be understood as appraisal mechanisms, which evaluate situations in relation to our plans and goals and lead to a readiness for action. In comics, the narrative context offers the situation to which the emotion then relates. The girl in the *Sinfest* comic for example is angry. This emotion evaluates the situation, namely that the insinuation of the boy is something that calls for a response, and it suggests her course of action, namely that she engages with him rather than carry on pontificating or stop talking altogether. Faces and emotions offer readers access into the mental operations that go on as characters encounter each other and as they evaluate events in relation to the stake they have in the situation.

panels, because we instinctively look at things other people are looking at. This is called the DEICTIC GAZE – a gaze that shows you something (see Butterworth 1995). In some instances, such as Figure 1.6, it can redirect your attention across panel boundaries.

Navigating the Comics Page

Let this image from *Desolation Jones* take you on a ride through a comics page. You begin reading in the top left corner, move to the right, then down a line and into the bottom right of the page. This is the basic reading direction, both of written texts and of comics. Conventionally, comics order their panels on the page in a grid of three by three or four by four panels, in which you move from the top left to top right in reading, then go down a line and repeat until you reach the end of the page (see for example Figure 5.6). This page from *Desolation Jones* both plays on and confounds this expectation. The panels are

Figure 1.6 Desolation Jones. From *Desolation Jones* © Warren Ellis and J.H. Williams III. Used with Permission of DC Comics.

superimposed onto each other, and there is no gutter but a background image underlying the entire page. Still, the central line that runs across the page, bright red in the original comic, outlines the reading path clearly.

There are numerous clues which help readers find their way through this comics page; the central line is only one among many. The deictic gazes of the characters are a second set of indicators. The speech bubbles and their reading direction are another, suggesting the movement which the readers' attention should take to make sense of the page. The movement begins, as we see the van from the front, and it ends, as we see the back of the vehicle move out of the frame. You can also follow the movement of the van itself, which travels from left to right in the first image, then down the diagonal, and then again from left to right in the bottom panels. As the characters are moved across the city, so you are moved across the face of the page by a great number of visual clues.

The page from *Desolation Jones* is structured into background and foreground. In the background, we have a city map of L.A. with the route of the van marked out as a red line. In the foreground, we have superimposed panels of the van and its passengers. While the background gives you a sense of the larger context, two characters moving across the city, the panels in the foreground give you the details of their conversation, their facial expressions, and their relation to each other. As you read a comics page, you move back and forth between background and foreground, between the general and the specific, in your inferences. Both the layout of the entire page and the details of the individual panels feed into a larger whole, a gestalt. "Gestalt" is a term from so-called "Gestalt psychology" which, at the beginning of the twentieth century, was interested in the way we intuitively chunk and group the information we perceive. The circle in Figure 1.2 illustrates the gestalt principle of closure.

Figure 1.7 illustrates a different process for forming a gestalt in perception: it can be either a vase, if you focus on the white, or a two facing profiles, if you focus on the black. You can never see both at the same time. What you see forms a closed whole, a gestalt. Still, you can switch between different gestalts and thereby reach a sense of the complexity of the image you see. This is also the case for the page from *Desolation Jones*. If you focus on the first panel, the red line is a sideline on the road. If you focus on the second panel, it is a reflection on Jones' sunglasses. If you focus on the background, it is a route on the map. If you focus on the last panel, it will be a sideline again.

The red line becomes many different things as you move your attention across the page. You focus on individual panels, which give you a moment of the action, and you process the information in the panels within the mental gestalt of this moment. As you move on across the page, however, you relate these

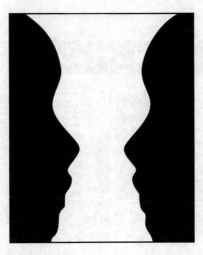

Figure 1.7   Rubin Vase.

moments to each other. The layout of the entire page, the way the panels relate to each other and the way they are arranged, is called "mise en page" in comics. Your attention as a reader fluctuates between a vague and general impression of the entire page and its composition and the specific gestalt of the event presented in a particular panel. This movement between background and foreground, between the part and the whole, creates a dynamic reading experience in comics, and it is the reason why both the unit of the panel and the unit of the page should be considered when analyzing comics.

Entering the Storyworld and Meeting its Participants

When you begin reading a comic, you take up clues from the page and construct a web of inferences from them. This web of inferences, however, is not free-floating. It is tied to the mental framework of a storyworld. A storyworld is the mental model you construct for the events which are represented in the panels. As you read, you redirect your attention from the real world into this fictional world. With more and more textual information, you elaborate and flesh out the storyworld, and you get a sense of what is likely to happen within it. Your inferences relate to the events in the storyworld, not to those in the real world.

Let's see how this works. Here are the first two pages of *V for Vendetta* (Figure 1.8). They take readers into the dystopian storyworld of a fascist Britain. The first panel gives you a basic exposition of the time and place: as the broadcast

Figure 1.8 V for Vendetta. From *V for Vendetta*. © DC Comics. Used with Permission.

Figure 1.8 (Cont'd) V for Vendetta. From *V for Vendetta*. © DC Comics. Used with Permission.

informs us, we are in London in the year 1997. The voice seems to be located in the building of "Jordan Tower," as the tail of the speech bubble suggests. Its ragged edges imply that the speech is transmitted electronically, a visual indicator that the language sounds not "round" but rough and fractured. The panel image lets us know that London in 1997 is not a happy place: large, featureless skyscrapers dominate the landscape, and it is dark and cloudy. As you continue reading through the page, you are taken to other places within the storyworld where the broadcast can be heard. The second panel shows people leaving a factory through a gate with a camera watching them. Nine o'clock is the time you finish work in this storyworld. Everyone seems to leave work at the same time, and the fences and camera seem to be the trappings of a repressive regime. The broadcast continues to predict the weather, tells people to avoid certain areas, reports increases in productivity, and a police raid. This broadcast is not news, but an instruction, a warning, and a demonstration that whoever issues them is in control of every aspect of these people's lives. In the third panel, we see a camera, monitoring the situation, and in the fourth policemen controlling traffic. The storyworld is now set up. It is a totalitarian world, whose denizens are under constant surveillance. From this set-up, you can expect certain narrative probabilities: someone will rise up against it, and the totalitarian regime will strike back and attempt to suppress this rebellion.

What is missing now are characters, fictional people who will set the narrative in motion. The following panels introduce these characters. We assume that both the girl and the man live in the same storyworld that has just been established. The girl's home seems average, whereas the man's abode is set up as an actor's dressing room with an illuminated mirror and film posters on the wall. While the girl seems fearful and uncertain, the man strides towards the mirror. The broadcast talks about rationing and food stuffs when we see the girl; we therefore assume that she is affected by lack of food. It talks about terrorists and suspects awaiting trials when we see the man; we can therefore assume that he is planning a subversive act. The silhouette of the open animal jaw in the top right corner suggests aggressiveness and the readiness to strike. The awaiting of trial could refer to a deadline, namely that the man will try to free the suspects, or that he will perform a trial for the regime itself. Much information about the two characters is communicated in these three panels. Even though the broadcast is probably not talking about them, as it places certain topics and terms within the panel's caption, we still connect these terms with the characters. They form part of our inference-making.

On the second page, the contrasting characterization of the girl and the man continues. Both are getting ready for an act which is probably illegal in this storyworld. The girl is putting on make-up and a short dress. She is probably going to solicit as a prostitute. By the final panel of this page, we know this to be the case. The page is a narrative unit in comics: it shows action potentials, such as the girl dressing up, and then brings them to a preliminary conclusion, such as the girl actually soliciting. At the same time, the final panel also raises a new question: how is the man going to react? Is he going to take up the offer? Is he going to reject? How will the girl react? Or is he maybe a government agent? The final panel of the page often leaves a gap that makes you go on to the next page to find an answer. Because we have seen two characters on these pages, we also wonder how these two characters are connected: do they know each other? Will they meet? Does the man set out to meet the girl? These questions remain in the back of our heads as we read on. They are part of the preconscious inferencing process, and you might not be aware of them. For your analysis of a comic, however, it makes sense to trace the inferences and spell out the questions and their answers.

The broadcast continues on the second page as well. In the first panel, it describes the outfit of "Queen Zara" as the girl looks down her own dress. The dress of the queen implies a proud display of couture, whereas the girl's unhappy look suggests that she is not sure that she is wearing (and doing) the right thing. As we draw our inferences, we connect and contrast the queen (or rather the stereotypical ideas we have about queens) with the girl. This highlights the insecurity of the girl. The process is that of METAPHORS: you think of something in terms of something else. Cognitive linguistics proposes that metaphors are mechanisms in which you project one thing (a king) onto another (a lion's heart) and compare their common features (probably courage). This panel works similarly, except that you take information from both the verbal discourse and the image: you compare the queen to the girl for her poise, self-assuredness, and the dignity of her fashion display. In contrast to a queen, the demeaning and pitiful situation of the girl is all the more striking.

In the following panels, this metaphorical process is used for a different purpose: irony. As the man's hand takes the mask, we read in the caption that one of the government officials instructs the population that "every man in this country [is] to seize the initiative and make Britain great again." Since the announcer talks about industry and economic prospects, we can infer that for him "making Britain great again" refers to productivity and work ethic. The man in the image seizes the mask, but he is probably not going to work in a factory. Rather, we infer that he is "seizing his own initiative" in a bid against the regime. His smiling mask, the bright lights and theatrical atmosphere go against everything the totalitarian regime stands for. For the man with the mask, "making Britain great again" carries a different meaning than for the announcer. The discrepancy between these meanings creates irony in the panel.

As we read through a comics page, we create a storyworld. This storyworld has basic features and probabilities, i.e. things that are likely to happen within it, and we draw our inferences within the framework of this storyworld. Characters are storyworld participants, and different things in the storyworld can mean different things to them. When we draw inferences, we try to relate these to characters and their intentions. These processes create a storyworld peopled with characters with different intentions, attitudes, and convictions. Comics can unfold a narrative in which many different voices interact. The Russian critic Mikhail Bakhtin (1981) calls the phenomenon of multivoiced narrative "HETEROGLOSSIA" and states that this is a key feature of the modern novel. It is also crucial to many comics and graphic novels which exploit the comics' medium's inherent juxtaposition of images and words. When you analyze comics, relate what you read to individual storyworld participants and ask yourself what it means to them. As I suggested at the beginning of this chapter, reading comics is not always straightforward, and their analysis needs to take into account the many different processes involved in making meaning from the lines and colors on the page.

Box 1.3   *Comics-Specific Signs and Conceptual Metaphors*

There is nothing that says "this is a comic" like a speech bubble, a SPEED LINE or an ONOMATOPOETIC EFFECT. These elements might not have their origin in the comics medium (see Chapter 5 for "proto-speech bubbles"), but comics have developed their narrative functions and often use them in their storytelling, and they are therefore often considered "comics-specific."

The speech bubble presents what a speaker says. Its tail points toward the speaker's mouth and locates what is said in the panel image. When this discourse cannot be located with a speaker in the panel image, it is represented in a caption, a box superimposed on the panel. When the discourse is not spoken, but only in the character's thoughts, the tail turns into a series of little dots, creating a THOUGHT

BUBBLE. The principle of the speech bubble, that is discourse emerging from a speaker's mouth and being directed at the listener, could be based on the CONCEPTUAL METAPHOR of "communication as conduit." Conceptual metaphors shape our way of thinking about something (see Lakoff and Johnson 2003); they can be discerned in verbal discourse but are also visually represented. Understanding the abstract notion of "communication" in the specific terms of a "conduit," we can try to "get the message across," "pack" our ideas into words, or "extract" meaning from a sentence. Speech bubbles show this conduit visually, and they are easy to understand because they draw on a conceptual metaphor which underlies the way we understand communication.

Speed lines are another comics-specific sign which show that a character moves very fast through space. They connect the space where the person stood before with the space where we can see them now. This implies that the character is moving so fast that their movement becomes a blur in our perception. Because we have a bodily conception of moving through space from a starting point to a goal (the so-called source-path-goal schema), we understand that the movement must be very fast. The aesthetic of the speed line is also connected to the rise of stop-motion photography at the beginning of the twentieth century, and it has been used in painting, such as Duchamp's *Nude descending a Staircase*. Comics sometimes feature visual signs connoting the emotional state of characters, like steam coming out of the character's ears when he is angry, or birds and stars to show bedazzlement. Some of these signs can be traced back to conceptual metaphors, like the steam to the conceptual metaphor that "anger is like a hot liquid in a container"; others seem more based on conventions.

Comics-specific signs, like speech bubbles and the visual signs I just discussed, are highly embodied pointers of action and provide shortcuts into the mental states of characters. Therefore, they have been singled out as signifying the infantile and hyperbolic nature of comics, and comics like *V for Vendetta* (that consider themselves to be serious narratives) tend to avoid them in favor of seemingly more subtle strategies of characterization and narration.

Comics Analysis – A Basic Checklist

✓ What is the spatial layout of the page? Does the mise en page follow the classical three by three pattern or does it suggest an alternative reading path? How does the comic strike a balance between the "pregnant moments" of the individual panels and the entire page?
✓ How do the characters relate to each other in the individual panels? How do their postures, gestures, and indicated movements underline the encounter? How do their bodies relate to each other across the page? What does the exchange of their deictic gazes tell you? How does this relate to the narrative?
✓ How do the facial expressions and the "pregnant moments" of the image relate to the dialogue as it unfolds in the speech bubbles?
✓ How does the comic establish the storyworld?
✓ Does the comic present different perspectives on the events? Does it juxtapose different takes on what happens in the storyworld through the combination of panels, or the combination of words and images within a panel?

Note

1 Lessing's original German term is "fruchtbarer moment," which is perhaps better translated as "critical" or "fruitful moment" (see the editor's notes in Lessing 1965, 275).

Recommended Reading

Bordwell, David. 1986. *Narration in the Fiction Film*. London: Methuen.

> The basic account of meaning-making in this chapter, namely, that we take up clues from the text and then draw inferences from them, is taken from David Bordwell's approach to films. *Narration in the Fiction Film* gives a basic outline of this approach; read his newer publications for the ways in which Bordwell has developed this account.

Grodal, Torben. 1997. *Moving Pictures: A New Theory of Film Genres, Feelings, and Cognition*. Oxford: Clarendon Press.

Johnson, Mark. 1987. *The Body in the Mind: The Bodily Basis of Meaning, Imagination and Reason*. Chicago: University of Chicago Press.

Arnheim, Rudolf. 2008. *The Power of the Center: A Study of Composition in the Visual Arts*. Berkeley: University of California Press.

These accounts outline the cognitive, emotional, and embodied approach, which underlies this chapter. Grodal presents an early model of embodied meaning-making in film, drawing on the cognitive sciences, while Johnson develops a larger aesthetic programme. Arnheim is an early account of embodied meaning-making and composition in the visual arts, first published in 1982.

Groensteen, Thierry. 2007. *The System of Comics*. Jackson: University of Mississippi Press.

Little, Ben. 2009. "Constructing the Reader's Perspective in *V for Vendetta*." *International Journal of Comic Art*, 11 1: 182–202.

Groensteen's basic outline of comics, their individual elements and how they work, offers a valuable introduction to the dynamics of the mise en page and spatial arrangement in comics. Little's article presents a detailed reading of *V for Vendetta*, and its effects on readers.

Jenkins, Jennifer M., Keith Oatley and Nancy Stein, eds. 1998. *Human Emotions: A Reader*. Oxford: Blackwell.

Gombrich, Ernst. 2002. *Art and Illusion: A Study in the History of Pictorial Representation*. London: Phaidon.

The *Human Emotions* reader presents an overview of contemporary psychological theories of emotions. Of particular interest are the articles by Ekman and Friesen, Oatley and Johnson-Laird, as well as Frijda. Ernst Gombrich's chapter on caricature discusses the impact of physiognomy and facial expression on our understanding of drawn characters. He explains "Töpffer's law," referring back to Rodolphe Töpffer's "Essay on Physiognomy," as the fact that we read a face always for its emotional expression.

Lessing, G.E. 1965. *Laokoön*, edited by Dorothy Reich. Oxford: Oxford University Press (several translations available).

Tucker, Brian. 2009. "Gotthold Ephraim Lessing's Laocoön and the Lesson of Comics." In *Teaching the Graphic Novel*, edited by Stephen Tabachnik, 28–35. Modern Language Association.

Lessing's essay distinguishes between the functions of time and space in the arts. A classic, but not unproblematic account. If you want to make your own way through Lessing's essay, Tucker's article, written from the perspective of a teacher, can be a helpful guide.

Forceville, Charles. 2005. "Visual Representations of the Idealised Abstract Concept Model of Anger in the Asterix Album *La Zizanie*." *Journal of Pragmatics*, 37.1: 69–88.

Forceville develops an account of conceptual metaphors in comics, in particular for the expression of anger.

References

Arnheim, Rudolf. 2008. *The Power of the Center: A Study of Composition in the Visual Arts*. Berkeley: University of California Press.

Bakhtin, Mikhail. 1981. *The Dialogic Imagination: Four Essays*. Edited by Michael Holquist. Austin: The University of Texas Press.

Butterworth, George. 1995. "Origins of Mind in Perception and Action." In *Joint Attention: Its Origin and Role in Development*, edited by Chris Moore and Patricia Dunham, 29–40. Hillsdale: Erlbaum.

Gallagher, Shaun. 2005. *How the Body Shapes the Mind*. Oxford: Oxford University Press.

Herman, David. 2002. *Story Logic: Problems and Possibilities of Narrative*. Lincoln: University of Nebraska Press.

Lakoff, George and Mark Johnson. 2003. *Metaphors We Live By*. Updated edition. Chicago: University of Chicago Press.

Lessing, G.E. 1965. *Laokoön*, edited by Dorothy Reich. Oxford: Oxford University Press (several translations available).

McCloud, Scott. 1994. *Understanding Comics: The Invisible Art*. New York: Harper Perennial.

Prince, Gerard. 1982. *Narratology: The Form and Function of Narrative*. Berlin: Mouton.

Töpffer, Rodolphe. 2003. *Essai de physiognomie*. Edited by Thierry Groensteen. Paris: Kargo.

Comics Discussed

Allison, John. 2009. *Bad Machinery*. Web. Last Accessed 28 Oct 2012.

Ellis, Warren. 2008. *Desolation Jones 1: Made In England*. Illustrated by J.H. Williams III. New York: DC Comics.

Ishida, Tatsuya. 2011. *Sinfest: Viva La Resitance*. Milwaukee: Dark Horse Books.

Moore, Alan. 2007. *V for Vendetta*. Illustrated by Dave Gibbons. New York: DC Comics.

Class Activity: Cut-up Comics

Get together in groups. Make two copies of a comic strip or a page-based comic. Cut up one of the copies into its individual panels and mix them. Exchange the cut-up comics between groups. Within your group, try to reconstruct the sequence of the comic strip of comic page and take into account the clues and the inferences possible between the panels. What other sequences are possible and how can you make sense of them? At the end of the exercise, compare your reassembled comic with the original and try to discuss why you might have chosen a different order.

A possible variation of this exercise would be a competition between groups with multiple cut-up comics, in which either (i) the greatest number of correctly reassembled comics or (ii) the greatest number of alternative, but feasible sequences are rewarded with a prize.

Writing Assignment 1

Go online and pick a web comic of your choice. Write a close-reading of this comic, going through it panel by panel. Describe the clues you pick up on, what kind of inferences you draw from them, and how they contribute to the narrative of the comic. Try to cover as many points from the checklist as you can and write 300–500 words.

Essay Question 1

Embodiment in Desolation Jones
Desolation Jones tells the narrative of a former MI5 agent, whose body has been marked by medical experiments. How is Jones' bodily experience represented in the comic? How are the bodily experiences of the other characters represented? How do their experiences and perceptions meet in their encounters? What kind of a story-world is communicated to readers through embodiment in page layouts (this has a much broader relevance in the comic than just Figure 1.6)?

Consider the composition of the pages, and the bodily postures and facial expressions of characters, in order to develop your analysis of what it means to have a body in the world of *Desolation Jones* – in relation to the character's experience of the storyworld, to their ability to move around within it and to the larger themes which the comic addresses.

2

The Way Comics Tell it: Narration and Narrators[1]

Comics present you with a number of visual and verbal clues which allow you to follow the PLOT, enter the storyworld, and engage with the characters. These clues are not placed at random, and they establish a relationship between you, as the reader, and the teller of the STORY, the narrator. Preliminarily, a narrative can be defined as a sequence of events, in which a number of characters engage and which is recounted by a narrator. This chapter will outline how comics use images and words to tell a story, how the telling and the story relate, how different kinds of narrators are established in comics, and it will conclude with a more general account of the cultural function of storytelling.

Showing and Telling

In his book *The Craft of Fiction*, Percy Lubbock writes:

"The art of fiction does not begin until the novelist thinks of his story as a matter to be *shown*, to be so exhibited that it will tell itself." (1965, 62)

Good fiction, Lubbock suggests, should be immediately accessible to the reader. The storyteller should retreat into the background and not intervene with excessive verbiage. In these lights, storytelling succeeds when readers see what is happening, but do not have the impression that anybody had told them what has happened. What does this mean for comics? Do they show in their images and tell in their words? And are those comics which have the least words the best?

Studying Comics and Graphic Novels, First Edition. Karin Kukkonen.

Lubbock's statement addresses two dimensions of storytelling: on the one hand, a story lets its readers enter a storyworld and invites them to engage with the characters and their fictional minds; on the other hand, a story always emerges from a constellation of clues which prompts readers to draw a particular set of inferences. A comic's narrative always has a certain rhetoric. This rhetoric can be related to an author or to a narrator, the instance we (might) project as telling the story to us. In comics, the narrator sometimes comes to the fore as a fully-fledged personality, but sometimes the narrative only implies an ordering agency that is not personalized. Literary studies in general, and narratology in particular, tend to avoid talking about the author, because we as readers can never be certain of the real intentions of the flesh-and-blood author. We will revisit the author in the chapter on autobiographical comics; in this chapter, we will talk of the narrator as the instance (within the comic) we project as telling the narrative.

Traditionally, it seems that images are better suited for the showing of a story, and words are better suited for the telling of a story. There is even some discussion as to whether images can narrate in the first place. In sequences, images can present different events which readers understand as part of a story, but also individual images can suggest a narrative, especially, when they represent the encounter between different characters or when they indicate several (sequential) events simultaneously. In comics, readers pick up clues from both the images and the words, and mostly, the two modes work together toward unfolding the comic's narrative in the panel sequence.

We have the elements of comics, words, images and sequence, assembled as features of the medium's storytelling now. And indeed, each of these elements contributes to comics' capacity for storytelling. Let's have a look at the first page of "Imperfect Hosts" from *The Sandman* to see how this works.

At the top of the page, we see a house in a Gothic landscape. The bats and gravestones suggest a setting in the horror genre. This image takes readers directly into the storyworld of this genre with its sudden scares and life-threatening encounters; it shows markers of the genre, and we as readers cast the storyworld accordingly. As Lubbock puts it, the narrative is "so exhibited that it will tell itself." The image holds the potential for a story, and because of our reading experience in the horror genre, we have a rough idea of what these potentials are. However, they remain potential, as nothing has happened yet. When we read the speech bubble, when we look over the entire page, a narrative emerges – clues are taken up and inferences are drawn from each of these elements.

Figure 2.1 The Sandman (I) From *Sandman Vol.1: Preludes and Nocturnes*.
© DC Comics. Used with Permission.

As Roland Barthes (1984) outlines, words can specify the meaning of an image – he calls this "anchorage." If we read "Wastelands, November 2011" in a caption next to the house, this would specify what we see in the image as being set in a particular time and space. Without the caption, the image could show any time and any space, and indeed, the home of Cain and Abel which we see here, is in a realm outside time and space. The dialogue in the speech bubbles anchors the image we see at a particular time and space, namely when the words are spoken, but it does not relate it to the storyworld at large. In most comics, as Barthes observes (1984, 11), words and images work as "RELAYS": they specify and describe each other. This use is employed in the second panel mid-left: Abel is staring at the present in front of himself, and from his facial expression, we see that he is afraid of it. His glance in the image specifies what the "it" in the speech bubble is, the thing he is afraid will explode. The words in the speech bubbles, on the other hand, specify what exactly he is afraid of (that it will explode) and why he is afraid (it is not his birthday and he does not trust his brother).

Words in comics are not necessarily tied to the telling, namely the explicating and specifying of the events and setting, but they can also show. Cain's choice of language, for example, shows his pompous attitude and his disrespect for his brother Abel, without the need for the narrator to tell us so. Images in comics are not necessarily tied to the showing either, namely the immediate present-ation of events; they can tell through their composition and the characters' bodies. Take the second image, in which both Cain and Abel look at the pre-sent, as an example. Here, Cain encroaches on the personal space of Abel, and Abel shrinks away from Cain and the present. The postures of the two brothers form a square, with their bodies as the two vertical lines and Cain's arm as the horizontal line. Abel's arm extending towards the present works as a diagonal across this square. The diagonal, a moment of dynamics in this rather stable composition, tells us about a moment of suspense – will he or will he not open the present?

Story, Discourse, and Plot

Abel, in the tradition of the victim of the horror film, is suspicious – he expects that the present will explode. Cain, in the tradition of the perpetrator of the horror film, is threatening – he wants to see his brother open the present. This is the basic question of the plot, the lines along which the action gets tangled up and along which it gets untied (the untying is also known as "DÉNOUEMENT").

The plot connects the events and actions in the story through the reasons we perceive for them and the effects they have. Abel is afraid of opening the present, because he does not trust his brother's stated reasons for giving him a present and he suspicious of what will happen once he opens it. The plot falls between what narratology, the study of narrative, calls story and what it calls discourse. The discourse is the text as it presents itself to the readers: the images, words, panel sequences, and page layouts of the comic itself. This is the *how* of storytelling. The story is the skeleton of events and encounters which discourse relates and fleshes out. It is the *what* of storytelling. The notions of story and discourse have been discussed in detail in narratology, and they give rise to a number of categories for storytelling which can also be applied to the storytelling in comics.

First, we don't necessarily read about the story events in the order in which they happened; there is a temporal discrepancy between discourse and story which occasions FLASHBACKS (the time of the discourse is after the story) and FLASHFORWARDS (the time of the discourse is before the story). The time it takes to recount an event might be longer than the event itself (for example a description of the explosion of the present), or it might be much shorter than it actually takes the event to unfold (for example the phrase "for thousands of years, Cain and Abel had lived together in this house"). Gérard Genette (1982) has written extensively on the relationship between discourse and story. He distinguishes (in terms of "tense") between order, which is the temporal discrepancy between story and discourse; duration, which is the extension or compression of discourse time in relation to story time; and frequency, which is the number of times a particular event is recounted.

Plot is the process that falls between story and discourse. As the French term for plot, "intrigue," suggests, it is what makes the story interesting, captivating, or downright scandalous to us. First discussed by Boris Tomashevsky (1965) and reconsidered by David Bordwell (1986) as "syuzhet" and by Raphaël Baroni (2007) as "intrigue," the plot is the arrangement of story events in the discourse, which shapes the ways in which readers construct the story from discourse by delaying information or making sudden revelations. Suspense, CURIOSITY, and SURPRISE all relate back to the temporal ordering of gaps in the plot (see Sternberg 1992). Narrativity has been defined as the difference between "the cat sat on the mat" and the "cat sat on the dog's mat" by Gerald Prince (1982), and this can be specified in relation to curiosity, suspense, and surprise. If readers know that the "cat sat on the dog's mat," they are in suspense about what will happen once the dog returns. They form projections about the future of the story, and their emotional involvement is guided by these. The mental operations of curiosity and surprise relate to gaps in the past of the story. When the dog returns to claim his mat, we might be surprised to recognize that the cat did not sit on its own mat (if the narrative left out this information) and we might be curious to find out the motivation of the cat for offending the dog (once it becomes obvious that we had insufficient information). In the example from *The Sandman*, the "dog's mat," the knot of the intrigue, is the present from Cain.

Each of the elements of the discourse of the comic's text has been put there for a reason – they all work as clues in the meaning-making process. However, they are not only there to point us towards the story, the what of narration. They pace the revelation of knowledge and they leave the readers in suspense, curiosity, and surprise. At the end of the page from *The Sandman*, readers have drawn a number of inferences concerning how the story is going to continue – they are in suspense. The final panel shows someone knocking on the door. This panel is separated from the main block of panels on the page and it is shown in a different color scheme. Visually, it represents a rupture with the previous events, and also on the level of the plot, the readers' current object of attention, the present, is replaced with a new one, the person behind the door. Now a new problem arises, new inferences emerge, the plot moves on, and a page is being turned.

Box 2.1   *Narrative Segments and Actors*

Narratology started as the endeavor to identify the basic structure of narrative, that is, the underlying features of storytelling. One set of these underlying features unfolds in time together with the narrative being told, the "narrative segments"; another set of underlying features are the agents which interact as the narrative progresses, the "narrative actors."

Regarding narrative segments, Tzvetan Todorov (1969) for example suggests that, on a very basic level, the "minimal complete plot" begins with the disturbance of an "equilibrium" and ends with its reestablishment. Narratives pose a problem and work towards its resolution. A more detailed account of narrative segments has emerged from linguistics and the analysis of oral storytelling with William Labov's (1999) six steps of "narrative structure." According to Labov, a narrative progresses through the following segments:

(1) Abstract. A preview of the narrative and what it's about. In Figure 2.2, Cain's suggestion to tell a "children's story" serves as an abstract.

(2) Orientation. Introducing the readers into the storyworld. Abel's description of the state before the world emerges and the introduction of the main characters serve as an orientation.

(3) Complicating action. The entanglement, problem or imbalance that gets the narrative going. The fight between Cain and Abel serves as a complicating action here, as do the alternative proposals of Death and Dream.

(4) Evaluation. Explaining what the point or purpose of the story is. Cain challenges Abel to prove the point of his story.

(5) Resolution. The conflict is cleared. Abel agreeing to Dream's offer, and living on as a storyteller in the world of dreams is the resolution.

(6) Coda. A conclusion to the story.

Elements from each of the segments may be missing, or be duplicated, in a particular story, but generally, the six steps construct a complete narrative.

The Russian fairy-tale scholar Vladimir Propp (1968) has identified thirty-one basic "functions" as narrative segments in storytelling (such as interdiction, and violation of interdiction, pursuit and rescue, etc.) which configure a tale. Propp groups his functions into "spheres" around particular character types, which are involved in several of these narrative segments. Such character types are hero, villain, dispatcher, helper, princess, father, donor and false hero. Propp's character types have been developed into a set of "actants", of narrative roles which can be found in any narrative, by Algirdas Greimas (2002). Note that the same character can take up different narrative roles, or that more than one character can take up one narrative role, depending on the situation. In Figure 2.2, Death and Dream for example both offer their services as helpers to Abel, and two characters thereby assume the same narrative role.

Box 2.2 *Serialization*

Comics are often published as comic books, which limits the number of pages available for each installment. Even though their narrative, as in *The Sandman*, might run across the entirety of a series, the individual installments each form a narrative unit. In the first issue of the *Sandman* series, Dream escapes from his imprisonment in a magician's coven in England. The issue ends with Dream's liberation and him cursing the man who imprisoned him with eternal waking. The problem introduced at the beginning of the issue (Dream is imprisoned) is resolved. Events of over seventy years are condensed into one issue, in which the discourse moves back and forth in time. The next issue, "Imperfect Hosts," follows on from this, but introduces a different unit of the narrative. It starts off with Cain and Abel, two characters who have not been introduced in the series yet, and it is set in a different world. However, readers expect that the different issues are connected into a larger narrative, and they might therefore guess who is knocking on the two brothers' door – it is Dream who seeks shelter after his escape.

The second issue spans its own narrative, in which Cain and Abel help Dream to revisit his realm and find out what he needs to do in order to regain control over it. It turns out that he has to find three artifacts of power he has lost, and this quest will be the subject matter of the following issues. The first volume of *The Sandman*, "Preludes and Nocturnes," connects the narratives of the individual issues together into the larger narrative of Dream's return and regaining of his power. Serialized narratives like *The Sandman* offer plots which have a complication at the beginning and a resolution at the end, but the resolution of each installment points forward to the complication of the next installment. The individual installments connect into a larger story arc, either through the enchainment of smaller plots or through introducing new characters or different perspectives on the same events. The publication format of the comic book accounts for the narrative peculiarities of serialization which comics share with TV series and feuilleton novels like Dumas' *Three Musketeers*.

The Narrator

So far we have been talking about the clues on the page and how they engage your minds as readers. Now we should turn our attention to the other side of this communicational exchange: who puts the clues there and with what intentions? Comics are created by writers, illustrators, inkers, and letterers. In some cases, such as *The Sandman*, each of these roles is taken up by someone different. In some other cases, such as the autobiographical comics we will address in the next chapter, one person does all of these jobs. For these purposes, we can talk of an author of the comic, who might be an individual or a collective of creators. Within the narrative, however, there is also someone who tells it. This is the narrator. Look at the following double page from *The Sandman*:

Here, Abel is the narrator. In the middle of the double page, we see a close-up of Abel's face. He begins the narrative in a speech bubble: "A long time ago, long before the world you know ..." This is a basic phrase to let readers know that a story begins now. The inferences are to be drawn in the framework of the new storyworld, rather than the main storyworld of the framing narrative, from here on in. For the rest of the panels, Abel's speech is inserted into a caption as he continues his story. What we see in the panels now is not Abel, but the storyworld he imagines and tells us about. Note how the style in which the world is drawn changes between the main storyworld and the storyworld of Abel's tale. His voice is not located in the space or the time of the storyworld; it is outside. Even when we see a version of Abel on the second page, his voice telling the story is not located in the same moment in time and it is therefore shown in captions. When Abel speaks in the storyworld he imagines, as in the penultimate panel, we see it as a speech bubble. Here, the different times of story and discourse are signaled through the interplay of speech bubbles and captions.

Narratologists distinguish between different kinds of narrators. I follow here the basic distinction between narrators located in the storyworld and narrators located outside of the storyworld. Genette's technical terms for these types similarly relate to "diegesis," meaning (roughly) storyworld: "HETERODIEGETIC" for narrators located outside the storyworld and "HOMO-DIEGETIC" for narrators in the storyworld. In the frame story of Cain and Abel in the library, we have a narrator outside of the storyworld. Somebody selects the sequence of events depicted, the image sizes and the perspective from behind the shelf, for example, but the comic does not mark out the

Figure 2.2 The Sandman (II). From *Sandman Vol. 6: Fables and Reflections*.
© DC Comics. Used with Permission.

Figure 2.2 (Cont'd)　The Sandman (II). From *Sandman Vol. 6: Fables and Reflections*.
© DC Comics. Used with Permission.

perspective as that of a narrator and locate him/her in the storyworld. The alternative to this would be a narrator in the storyworld who tells the story from a first-person perspective. In the children's story, we have Abel as a narrator, who tells a story with himself as the main character, but he distances himself from the narrative by using the third person in the captions, and by speaking of himself as "Abel" instead of "I." Abel is a homo-diegetic narrator who poses as a heterodiegetic narrator, perhaps in the convention of children's tales, perhaps in order to distance himself from the traumatic events he recounts.

Abel is a also PERSONALIZED NARRATOR, a narrator who has been introduced in some detail to the reader. This kind of narrator is common in the genre of horror comics, to which *The Sandman* refers frequently. In the classical EC horror comics (more on their historical relevance in chapter 5), there are three such narrators, the Old Witch, the Crypt Keeper and the Vault Keeper. On the following page, you see how they were used in the 1950s.

This is the final page of a story told by the Old Witch. You can read the discourse of the narrator in the captions. Up to the fourth panel, the written text does not mark whether the narrator is homo- or heterodiegetic. In the fifth panel, the pronoun "I" appears and readers know that the narrator must be located in the storyworld because she "opens a door," which has an effect on the lighting of the image. Only then, in the far right of the panel, do we see the narrator's "Heh!" in the speech bubbles, which serves as a further indicator that the narrator stands just outside the panel frame. In the last two panels, we finally see her in the storyworld, interacting with the children. From an ambiguous situation, in which we assume a heterodiegetic narrator, we (and the children) suddenly find confirmation to the suspicion that the narrator is right there in the storyworld, and this contributes to the shock and surprise ending of the story.

The Old Witch fulfills all three functions which Marie-Laure Ryan (2001) has identified for the narrator: (i) she creates the storyworld for readers (creative function); (ii) she communicates the events of the story to readers (transmissive function); (iii) she testifies to the authenticity of the story (testimonial function). The Old Witch does something more, too: she also reflects on the fact that she is the narrator of the story when she addresses the reader openly (both through her glance and through the "you" in the last panel), and when she mentions the genre and publication format the story appears in. This is called METANARRATION. Metanarration points the readers' attention to the fact that the storyworld is (i) created and (ii) communicated

Figure 2.3 Shock Suspenstories. EC logo™ and image © Wm. M. Gaines, Agent, Inc. 2012. All rights reserved.

by the narrator, and through this it threatens to undo the (iii) authenticity of the story. The Old Witch, however, places herself in her own narrative at the same time, thereby attesting to its authenticity. All the different kinds of narrators – homo- or heterodiegetic and personalized or DEPERSONALIZED NARRATOR – can be assessed through Ryan's functions of creation, transmission, and testimony.

There has been some debate as to whether, apart from personalized narrators like the Old Witch or Abel, there is a narrator in visual media like films and comics at all. As David Bordwell puts it, in a visually represented storyworld, quite often, there is "no place for the narrator to hide" (1986, 111). Indeed, in the frame story telling us about Cain and Abel, there is no ready spatial position for the narrator. The Old Witch's game of hide-and-seek in the EC comic, on the other hand, constitutes the twist of the story. She leaves her traces in the discourse until she suddenly comes to the fore. Even in the example of Abel's story, the situation is presented in a particular way, and the clues on the page guide us towards constructing it in a particular fashion. The destabilized shelf in the left-hand background points towards the dynamics of the situation, the strong change of perspective changes the pacing of the story, and the close-up on Abel's face suggest that something personal is to follow. As Bordwell proposes in his account of film narration, narration unfolds as we configure the story from the clues. For Bordwell, this means that film has a narration, but not necessarily a narrator. Indeed, the narrator is not necessarily cued as a person (like Abel and The Old Witch), but as an instance, the narrator is always implicit in the narration through the arrangement of the clues and the way this arrangement guides readers across the page. In the first example page from *The Sandman*, the narrator does not come to the fore, but the arrangement of the panels, and the gap before the final panel are clearly traces of a narrator shaping the narration.

Narration, Focalization, and Point of View

So far, we have addressed the narrator as readers' projection of the person who creates, transmits and testifies to the authenticity of the narrative. Abel as narrator also seems to create the images, and clues he presents to readers. The perspective of the images, however, is not necessarily related to a particular person's experience or spatial position. We can distinguish here between narrators, and their narration, FOCALIZERS, and their focalization, and OBSERVERS and their point of view. In what follows, I will give a rough outline on how these three different roles can be distinguished for comics. There has been a lot of debate around narration, focalization and its overlaps, and many narratologists might disagree with my account. It is meant to be useful for a basic analysis, rather than a flawless system.

For the distinction between narration and focalization, take Abel's story in *The Sandman*: We clearly know that this is Abel's tale from the look of the images and from the way he tells his story, even though he distances himself by using the third-person pronoun. *The Sandman* presents the story through Abel's focalization. According to Gérard Genette (1982), narration refers to the voice that speaks; focalization refers to the perspective from which the narrative is recounted. As readers, we share the knowledge of the focalizer and partake in his or her experience. However, who speaks and who experiences are not necessarily the same thing. You might have a third-person depersonalized narrator, but this narrator might only present knowledge and experience that are accessible to one of the characters. You might have a first-person character narrator who tells you things which this character cannot know. Focalization is the perspective to which the text limits the knowledge we get about the storyworld.

For comics, we have a problem here – the visual perspective of the image and the narrative perspective of focalization do not always match. We see Abel acting in the images which he focalizes (see Figure 2.2). In order to account for this problem, focalization can be reconsidered in terms of "knowledge about the storyworld." The knowledge we get about the storyworld of the children's tale is limited to Abel's perspective. The images however, are presented from a neutral point of view: we see Cain and Abel fight in the foreground of the first image of the second page, but we do not ask from whose actual point of view it is shown. Still, Abel's focalization of the story is clear, as the narrative discourse talks in general terms about "fighting" and neglects to specify the brutality of the encounter and its outcome, and as the events are presented in a cute drawing style, which distracts from the murder it recounts. To reiterate, the spatial point of view of the image is usually not cued as relevant in comics. There are some cases, however, when the point of view of the image is made salient, for example through point-of-view editing (see the box on "CONTINUITY EDITING"). In these instances, the observer is cued, but comics tend not to sustain such points of view over long stretches of narrative. We will come back to the observer in the chapter on autobiographical comics.

Box 2.3   *Image Sizes and Angles*

For discussing the individual panel images and the relation between the section of the storyworld we see and its relation to the storyworld itself, it is useful to consider the vocabulary film studies have developed for image sizes and angles. By choosing a particular image size and angle, the comic presents you with a clue on how the story is to be perceived. There are four basic image sizes in film (see Figure 2.2 for reference):

- Long shot (the top panel on the second page). You see the entire scene with the characters from a distance.
- Medium long shot (the third and forth panel on the second page). It shows the acting characters in their entirety or most of their bodies.
- Medium shot (the final panel of the second page). The upper body and the hand gestures of the characters can be seen in detail; the setting becomes less relevant.
- Close up (the shot of Abel's face on the first page when he starts telling the story). Details of the object are visible and, often, the focus is on the character's facial expression.

In addition to shot sizes, you can also detect the angle of the image. Usually, this is on the level of the characters' eyes (eye-level angle). Sometimes, however, the image can be framed from a low angle (frog's eye) or from a high angle (bird's eye). The EC comic (Figure 2.3) uses a switch from low to high angle framing to underline the manifestation of the homodiegetic narrator between the fourth and fifth panel.

What is shown in a comic's image is usually carefully selected in terms of framing (image size and angle). In the last three panels of the Cain and Abel story, for example, you see first Abel with Death, the little girl, then with Dream and Death and then just with Dream. In the last panel, Death disappears. This makes sense when you consider how the selection of the shot contributes to the storytelling: at first, Death approaches Abel and offers to take him into her garden. Then Dream makes his offer, and Abel stands between Death and Dream. When Abel considers Dream's offer and is finally convinced by it, Death literally drops out of the picture.

Box 2.4   Continuity Editing

Films combine their individual shots in editing. Classical Hollywood Cinema has developed a style of editing which ties into our (spatial) perception so well that we get a sense of narrative continuity just from the arrangement of the shots. It is called "continuity editing." Comics often use conventions of continuity editing as well when combining panels, even though they do not create the continuous flow of film (see the section on closure in Chapter 1). The individual images in the panels present "pregnant moments" of the events. We rarely read comics images as one-to-one representations of different stages of the events, but as sets of clues for salient features of the story. Still, panels are often arranged similar to the shot sequences of film. Keeping this in mind, the terminology from film studies is useful for comics analysis as well.

Here are two of the basic conventions of continuity editing: point-of-view editing and the 180-degree rule.

Point-of-view-editing is one of the ways in which images can highlight the observer, i.e. the instance from whose spatial position an image is perceived. There are three shots involved: the first shows you who is looking, the second what he/she is seeing and the third how the onlooker reacts. Sometimes, the first shot (who is looking) is missing and this can create suspense because we sense that this is someone's point of view, but we do not know where in the storyworld it is located. Sometimes, the final shot which gives the reaction is missing.

When films show a dialogue, they usually alternate between the partners in the conversation, showing first the one and then the other. If you draw a line between the two partners in conversation, the camera tends to stay on one side of it, moving from overshoulder view to overshoulder view. This is called the 180-degree rule. In the last three panels of Figure 2.2, for example, the images show the exchange between Abel, Dream, and Death from the same line, moving from the right of the field to the center, and then on to the left. As Abel makes his decision, the vantage point of the images (what would be the camera in film), pivots around him. In the two *Sinfest* comics (Figures 1.1 and 1.4), the 180-degree rule is violated, creating the impression of a rupture in the narrative flow. If you look closely at the relative positions of characters and consecutive positions from which the images are taken, you might find that the 180-degree rule is often violated in comics. Mostly, however, this violation is not noticed in reading comics (because we do not seem to reconstruct a "film" of the events between panels).

Narrative as Meaning-Making

We find stories not just in the fictional narratives of comics, films, and novels. In decidedly fact-based genres and media environments like journalism, history-writing, and the courtroom, stories shape our meaning-making. Stories underlie the way we communicate our experience of the world and the way our cultures make sense of their history and their present. Narrative in this capacity can be defined as a process which establishes causal connections between events, which introduces agency and intentions for characters and which suggests that there is a "point" (a term from Labov 1999) which makes the story worth telling. *The Sandman*, a long-running comics series, gives many different examples of how we create, individually and collectively, meaning through narrative patterns.

In *The Sandman* the theatrical career of William Shakespeare is reinterpreted: Shakespeare made a deal with Dream, who gives him access to the deepest dreams of mankind in exchange for two plays. The hapless young actor and playwright turns into a successful star of the Elizabethan stage. Gaiman does not simply outline the career of Shakespeare, but his narrative establishes a causal explanation for his success. As E.M. Forster observes, in the narrative kernel "the king died and then the queen died of grief," the causal connector "of grief" is the most important (2005, 87). Causality and the agency and intentions of characters are closely connected: Shakespeare wants to become a successful playwright, and he therefore strikes a deal with Dream. Dream wants to give the world some idea about his workings, he wants to impress the fairy queen Titania, and he therefore offers the deal to Shakespeare. By adding causality and agency to Shakespeare's career course, Gaiman makes these events tellable, he gives them a "point." When the pay-back becomes imminent, the story arrives at a crisis, and this is the moment when Gaiman has the narrative discourse begin.

The Sandman revisits narrative patterns throughout mythology, history, religion and popular culture, and thereby highlights that stories are every-where in human culture. Stories are important to us as human beings, because they allow us to make meaning from the world as it presents itself to us and to communicate that meaning. As cognitive approaches to literature suggest, not only do stories help us make sense of what has happened but also of what might happen: by imagining alternative scenarios, we can reason through problems and find solutions without having to put ourselves in danger. Narrative patterns allow us to connect events into meaningful wholes and into complexes of intentions and agency to which we can relate and which we can evaluate. Perhaps not all thinking is shaped by the causality, agency and tellability of stories, but they help us to understand and communicate what happened when, where, and why.

* * *

Comics are, generally speaking, a narrative medium – they tell stories. Their words, images, and their arrangement in sequences and page layouts create a story. This narrative unfolds from complication to resolution, between story, discourse and plot, and narrator, focalizer and observer can feature when the story is communicated to readers. When you consider the narrative of a comic, you look into the connections between the clues and the uses to which they are put. Stories can be "exhibited so as to tell themselves" as Lubbock suggests, but there is always a set of rhetorical strategies at work.

Graphic Narrative – A Basic Checklist

✓ Identify elements of "showing" and "telling" in the panels. How do the comic's modes of images and words contribute to these narrative activities?

✓ How are story and discourse related to each other? Does the discourse reorganize the order of the story events? Which story event does it begin with? Does it retell story events more than once? What is the rhetorical effect of this organization?

✓ What is the crucial conflict of the story? How does it find its dénouement? Can you identify the narrative segments?

✓ Does the narrative work with curiosity, suspense and surprise?

✓ What type of narrator do you have? How does the narrator deal with the creative, communicative and authenticating functions? How can you discern the rhetoric of the narrator? Where does she leave her traces? Consider images sizes, image angles, and drawing style (among other things).

✓ Can you identify a particular focalization in the text? Can you identify an observer and her point of view?

Note

1   With apologies to David Bordwell. 2006. *The Way Hollywood Tells It: Story and Style in Modern Movies*. Berkeley: University of California Press.

Recommended Reading

Miller, Ann. 2007. *Reading Bande Dessinée: Critical Approaches to French Language Comic Strip*. Bristol: Intellect. Ch.6. Bande dessinée and narrative theory.
Herman, David. 2009. *Basic Elements of Narrative*. Oxford: Wiley-Blackwell.
Groensteen, Thierry, 2011. *Bande dessinée et narration*. Paris: PUF.
Gardner, Jared and David Herman, eds. 2011. *Graphic Narratives and Narrative Theory*. Special issue of *SubStance* 40 1.

These accounts concern themselves specifically with the applications of narrative theory to comics and its problems.

Bordwell, David. 1986. *Narration in the Fiction Film*. London: Methuen.
Fludernik, Monika. 2006. *An Introduction to Narratology*. Abingdon: Routledge.
Herman, David. 2002. *Story Logic: Problems and Possibilities of Narrative*. Lincoln: University of Nebraska Press.

Three key overview works on narrative theory: Bordwell lays the foundations of a narrative theory of film (and visual media). Fludernik offers an introduction to the manifold accounts of narrative which narratology offers. Herman presents narratology from a cognitive point of view, discussing storyworlds and pointing towards the larger cultural functions of storytelling.

Branigan, Edward. 1992. *Narrative Comprehension and Film*. London: Routledge.
Genette, Gérard. 1982. *Figures of Literary Discourse*. Oxford: Blackwell.
Horstkotte, Silke and Nancy Pedri. 2011. "Focalisation in Graphic Narratives." *Narrative*, 19.3: 330–57.
Mikkonen, Kai. 2008. "Presenting Minds in Graphic Narratives." *Partial Answers*, 6.2: 301–21.
Ryan, Marie-Laure. 2001. "The Narratorial Functions: Breaking Down a Theoretical Primitive." *Narrative*, 9: 146–52.
Sternberg, Meir. 1992. "Telling in Time (II): Chronology, Teleology, Narrativity." *Poetics Today*, 13.3: 463–541.
Labov, William. 1999. "The Transformation of Experience in Narrative." In *The Discourse Reader*, edited by Adam Jaworski and Nicolas Coupland, 221–35. London: Routledge, 1999.
Barthes, Roland. 1984. "The Rhetoric of the Image." In *Image – Music – Text*, 32–51. London: Fontana.

These books and articles outline different aspects of narrative, and narrative and comics. Branigan, Genette, Horstkotte and Pedri as well as Mikkonen tackle the issue of focalization. Ryan addresses the function of the narrator. Sternberg looks into surprise, curiosity, and suspense (in the third section of his paper), Labov outlines six steps in narrative sequence, and Barthes talks about the different relations between images and words in meaning-making.

Bordwell, David. 1988. "The Classical Hollywood Style, 1917–1960." In *The Classical Hollywood Cinema: Film Style and Mode of Production to 1960*, edited by David Bordwell, Janet Staiger and Kristin Thompson, 1–84. London: Routledge.

David Bordwell and Kristin Thompson. 2004. *Film Art: An Introduction*. 7th edition. Boston: McGraw Hill.

Bordwell's section on "Continuity Editing" offers an introduction to the topic from a cognitive perspective. *Film Art* introduces technical terms from film, such as shot sizes and angles.

H. Porter Abbott. 2008. *The Cambridge Introduction to Narrative*. 2nd edition. Cambridge: Cambridge University Press.

Abbott's introduction discusses in detail the social relevance of narrative and its importance in meaning-making outside fiction.

References

Baroni, Raphaël. 2007. *La Tension Narrative: Suspense, Curiosité et Surprise*. Paris: Seuil.

Barthes, Roland. 1984. "The Rhetoric of the Image." In *Image – Music – Text*, 32–51. London: Fontana.

Bordwell, David. 1986. *Narration in the Fiction Film*. London: Methuen.

Forster, E.M. 2005. *Aspects of the Novel*. Harmondsworth: Penguin.

Genette, Gérard. 1982. *Figures of Literary Discourse*. Oxford: Blackwell.

Greimas, Algirdas. 2003. *Sémantique structurale: recherche de méthode*. 3rd edition. Paris: PUF.

Labov, William. 1999. "The Transformation of Experience in Narrative." In *The Discourse Reader*, edited by Adam Jaworski and Nicolas Coupland, 221–35. London: Routledge, 1999.

Lubbock, Percy. 1965. *The Craft of Fiction*. London: Jonathan Cape.

Prince, Gerald. 1982. *Narratology: The Form and Functioning of Narrative*. Berlin: Mouton.

Propp, Vladimir. 1968. *Morphology of the Folktale*. 2nd edition. Austin: University of Texas Press.

Ryan, Marie-Laure. 2001. "The Narratorial Functions: Breaking Down a Theoretical Primitive." *Narrative*, 9: 146–52.

Sternberg, Meir. 1992. "Telling in Time (II): Chronology, Teleology, Narrativity." *Poetics Today*, 13.3: 463–541.

Todorov, Tzvetan. 1969. "Structural Analysis of Narrative." *Novel: A Forum on Fiction*, 3.1: 70–6.

Tomashevsky, Boris. 1965. "Thematics." In *Russian Formalist Criticism: Four Essays*, edited by Lee Lemon and Marion Reis, 61–95. Lincoln: University of Nebraska Press.

Comics Discussed

Gaiman, Neil. 1995. *The Sandman 1: Preludes and Nocturnes*. Illustrated by Sam Keith, Mike Dringenberg and Malcolm Jones III. New York: DC Comics.

Gaiman, Neil. 1993. *The Sandman 3: Fables and Reflections*. Illustrated by Jill Thomson et al. New York: DC Comics.

Ingels, Graham. 2006 (1953). "Sugar 'N Spice 'N …." *Shock Suspenstories*. Vol. 1 Issues 1–6, 205–211. Timonium: Gemstone Publishing.

Class Activity 2: Tall Tales

Take the first feature or capacity you can think of, either mental or physical. Imagine this feature or capacity in terms of a superpower, amplifying its scope or force. Now identify the uses this superpower can be put to in an encounter between characters. What could be the larger plot complications this feature gives rise to? How can they be resolved? How can you implement suspense, surprise, and curiosity in your narrative? Can you think of any particular use of narrator, focalizer, or observer to render your tall tale more interesting or more intensely felt by the reader? Outline your narrative in bullet points, discuss it with other members of your group and present your "tall tale" in class.

Writing Assignment 2

Take a short comics sequence (2–3 pages). Identify the narrator, the point of view of the images and the focalization from which the story is told. Identify the relation between the discourse and the story, as well as the points at which the plot is complicated and at which it is resolved, and how clues (like size and perspective of images, as well as panel combinations) contribute to the build-up of suspense, curiosity, or surprise in the plot. Write about 300–500 words.

Essay Question 2

Story, Myth and History in The Sandman
We have talked about *The Sandman* in terms of narrative as a means of cultural meaning-making in the final section of this chapter. Consider on a broader scale how the series uses this function of narrative, when it retells stories familiar from myth and history. What different traditions can you distinguish? How does the series change these stories? How does it combine them into its own, larger narrative? How does this relate to the general features of meaning-making through storytelling?

Consider both the stories themselves (such as Orpheus' tale) and their modes of storytelling and genre (such as the multiple narratives of Chaucer's *Canterbury Tales* or tragedy in *The Kindly Ones*).

3

Narrating Minds and Bodies: Autobiographical Comics

Autobiographical comics are a key genre in the medium of comics. Through words, images, and sequences, autobiographical comics tell of the personal experience of the children of Holocaust survivors (*Maus*), the experience of relating to one's father (*Fun Home*), or the awkwardness of growing up (*Blankets*). This chapter introduces autobiographical comics, how they establish the subjectivity of experience, how they assert the authenticity of their narrative and how they reflect on the very process of telling their story.

Style and Subjectivity

In Abel's narrative in *The Sandman*, readers get a glimpse of Abel's imagination: his retelling of the story of Cain and Abel is based on a particular set of assumptions (his sacrifice of a goat pleased god because it was "white and fluffy"), and it is presented in a distinct visual style. The pleasant, sweet worldview of Abel is represented in the cute, manga-like rendition of the characters and the story-world. Here, images and words work together to show the fictional mind of Abel and his experience of the world to us.

Because comics work with drawn images, not photographs, and because they are often lettered by hand as well, what we see on the page tends to communicate a particular style. Most comics readers recognize a comic by Will Eisner, Jack Kirby, or Chris Ware by the distinct drawing style in the images, the distinct ways of presenting the page layout and the distinct ways of lettering. Traces of the author can be found not only in the rhetorical strategies of placing clues for meaning-making on the page, but also in the very style of these clues. Some

Studying Comics and Graphic Novels, First Edition. Karin Kukkonen.
© 2013 John Wiley & Sons, Ltd. Published 2013 by John Wiley & Sons, Ltd.

styles use many strokes and appear busy, like Robert Crumb's late style; others are simple and appear elegant, like Herge's use of "ligne claire." The visual style of a panel works towards what Philippe Marion (1993, 151–60) calls "GRAPHIA-TION": the lines, contours and colors constitute the gesture of enunciation in the drawing. Graphiation gives us an idea of what the creator of these images is like.

Even though I have introduced graphiation through examples of real authors such as Crumb and Ware, it can be extended beyond flesh-and-blood creator of the pages you see. The images in the Cain and Abel story were not drawn by Abel, but by the artist Jill Thompson. Still, they serve as "graphiation," as a person-based enunciation, of Abel's imagination. In autobiographical comics, the assumption is that the author tells a story about him- or herself, and that the general "graphiation" of the drawing style is his or her personal expression of experience.

Because comics, unlike printed books, are hand-drawn, they seem to work as an immediate representation of the experience of the author both for what is being said, that is the events we see on the page and the dialogue we read, and for how it is being said, that is the look and style of the material on the page. Comics scholars therefore often use the term "AUTOGRAPHY" for autobiographical comics. Autography, going back to the Greek words for "self" and "writing, drawing," implies that the author draws him- or herself, whereas autobiography refers to the traditional written genre, which does not imply a connection to visual style.

Box 3.1   *Underground, Independent, and Alternative Comics*

Autobiographical comics have their roots in the underground and alternative comics which have emerged outside mainstream comics publications, such as humorous strips or SUPERHEROES, though they may occasionally refer back to these genres (such as Chris Ware's *Jimmy Corrigan* to the superhero comics or Art Spiegelman's *Maus* to the funny animal tradition). UNDERGROUND COMICS in the 1960s were part of the countercultural movement, when journals like Robert Crumb's *Zap Comix* (1968) or *Help!* (1960) were launched outside the mainstream distribution mechanisms of comics and ignoring censor-ship restrictions (more on this in Chapter 5). Underground comics, or "comix" as they came to be called, were creator-owned and soon came to be understood as a medium of self-expression. This self-expression would lead to a strong focus on autobiographical narratives, perhaps most famously in Justin Green's *Binky Brown Meets the Holy Virgin Mary* (1972), and the *American Splendor* series (1976–2008), written by Harvey Pekar and illustrated by many different comics artists.

INDEPENDENT COMICS are similarly creator-owned comics which are published outside the main publishing houses, but which follow a (largely) professional publication schedule. An example of such independent comics is Dave Sim's series *Cerebus the Aardvark* (1977–2004). What counts as an "independent" comic is rather difficult to define; in some instances it can be extended to cover the entire comic's production not coming from DC and Marvel. Similarly difficult to pin down in a precise definition are alternative comics. Alternative comics are creator-driven and owned, and not necessarily connected to the counterculture, like underground comics were. They offer an alternative to the mainstream, which means, on the one hand, that they reject mainstream formulae and embark on ambitious projects (such as Spiegelman's *Maus*), and on the other hand, that they diversify their graphic styles and look at comics narratives outside the Anglophone sphere (Spiegelman and Mouly's magazine *RAW* (1980–91), in which *Maus* was first published, for example featured French artists as well). Much of the current reevaluation of comics as a worthwhile subject of study is due to alternative comics and the appreciation they have enjoyed since the 1980s.

Autographic Agents

Unlike the story within a story which Abel tells, we as readers expect that the main character of an autobiography is the same person as the author and the narrator. Philippe Lejeune (1989) calls this tacit agreement the "AUTOBIOGRAPH-ICAL PACT." This can be extended to include focalization: if the perspective of a focalizer is highlighted in the images, they are assumed to be focalized from his or her point of view. As we have seen in the previous chapter, the perspective of a comic's image does not need to be shown from the visual point of view of the focalizer. Such a visual point of view can be cued, but more commonly, the image uses an outside perspective which shows what the focalizer knows at this point in time and, more particularly, what is important to him or her. A page from Alison Bechdel's *Fun Home* will shed some light on these distinctions:

Figure 3.1 Fun Home. From FUN HOME: A Family Tragicomic by Alison Bechdel. © 2006 by Alison Bechdel. Used by Permission of Houghton Mifflin Harcourt Publishing Company. All rights reserved.

Alison is the first-person narrator of the verbal discourse atop the panels. She is also the focalizer of the panel images, even though we see her in all the images. Focalization means here that the images do not literally represent what Alison sees at this point, but how she imagines it in hindsight. In the first panel, when she introduces her girl-friend, we see her mother with a skeptical expression and her father quizzical and expectant. The image presents the clues as placed there by Alison to recapture her memory of that moment. The narrator in the present remembers the past and tells us about it. Alison features in both these moments, but she is split into an Alison in the past (the girl in the image) and the Alison of the present (the narrative voice and the drawer and focalizer of the image). Sometimes, this distinction between the two selves of the auto-graphic narrator is hidden, as in the first panel, sometimes, it is brought to the fore, as in the second panel, where a caption with an arrow is inserted into the image with the ambiguously ironic words "heart and soul." Here, the Alison of the present comments on the experience of the Alison of the past.

In terms of point of view, none of the images could have been perceived by the Alison of the past. Still, the final panel makes Alison's perception salient. This panel has the same visual perspective on the events as the second panel above it; it shows Alison and her father playing the piano. The third panel locates this point of view in the storyworld as being placed in the window of the Bechdels' living room. In the second and third panel, this location is not marked. In terms of continuity editing, we are given a belated establishing shot of the scene; a long shot after a medium shot in the panel before. In the final panel, however, the spatial position is marked: we see the frames and the shutters of the window, as well as the glass which separates the observer from the events. The point of view is placed outside the house, and we are separated from the events inside it. Alison's verbal discourse ("But not close enough.") underscores this separation. Bechdel embodies the position of the observer at various points in the comic, when she makes the physical point of view of the image salient, and thereby gives readers an immediate sense of the situation.

This leaves us with three different autographic agents which can be read from the clues in the image and its perspective: the narrator, who creates the image; the focalizer, on whose knowledge it is based; and the observer, whose embodied spatial position is represented and which the reader is invited to share. In this final panel, Bechdel places readers outside the living room to make them experience her own sense of displacement from her family. Narrator, focalizer, and observer all come together. However, it is certainly not the case that each of these autographic agents need to be cued in each of the panels. There can be panels in which no narrative voice is given; there can be panels in which no particular focalization is suggested; and there can be panels in which the observer position is not marked. These distinctions between autographic agents are not meant to be a checklist, but to help you keep track of the different ways in which author and narrator can be brought to the fore in the autobiographical comic.

Embodiment

When Alison Bechdel cues us to imagine the physical position of the observer in the storyworld, she makes her spatial relation to the events salient to us by putting readers in her spot. This is an instance of embodiment through the displacement of the observer's perspective. Craig Thompson's *Blankets* creates a very different sense of embodiment: he does not push us away but draws us in. Let's have a look at Blankets (fig. 3.2; on pp. 62–3):

We see Craig and Raina, the main character and his first love, in an intimate conversation. Each of the images is a still image presenting one moment in time. The first image shows Raina lying on the left. In the second image, we have a close-up of her, lying vertically. It is as if she had moved between the two panels by about ninety degrees. In the last panel of the page, we have a repetition of this image from a higher angle. On the following page, she and Craig lie as if upside down from the first panel. Raina's half-circle is complete. The changing angles of these images create the illusion that Raina and Craig are rotating. As we discussed in the first chapter, the cognitive sciences suggest that we also unconsciously experience the movements we perceive. This page presents only an illusion of movement, since the two bodies actually lie still. However, our bodily sense of orientation, our body schema, is destabilized, and we might experience a slight drift as we look at the shifting bodies in these images. The round shapes of the candles in the first and last panel, the lack of orienting background and the movements of Raina's arms towards Craig reinforce this impression.

As their conversation begins at the top of the page, Raina's movement gets going. After their conversation has come to an end, and their hands interlock, the swirl of movement comes to a halt as well. But if Raina's half-circle seems to be a smooth movement, Craig's is not. Raina in the first panel faces towards the direction in which she will fall, and her hands form a half-circle, whereas Craig lies rather stiffly against the grain of the movement with his hands apart. The third panel, which shows only Craig, presents his arms in an awkward position, which interrupts the flow of the movement. Between the penultimate and the last panel, he finally turns toward Raina, and their hands meet. There are two levels of embodiment unfolding here: on the one hand, the illusion of movement coming from the manipulation of the angle of the image; on the other hand, the actual postures of the bodies of the two characters. The relative positions of the bodies, their gestures and their movement, or rather the illusion of their movement, tell us about the ways in which this situation is experienced by its protagonists. Raina's experience seems effortless and smooth, whereas Craig seems self-conscious and stiff. Thompson uses embodiment here to help readers participate in his own experience of his awkwardness and Raina's perceived grace in this situation, as well as the final harmony in their encounter.

This sense of experience is given through the bodies of the characters and their arrangement on the page. Embodiment in comics can give the experience of an entire scene as in *Blankets*, or it can render a sudden sense embodied (dis) placement when the observer comes to the fore as in *Fun Home*. When you look for embodiment in comics, think of the spatial position in relation to the parameters of the storyworld – is the change of perspectives smooth or is continuity editing disrupted? Think of the relative movements of the characters in the panels and on the page as a whole – what is the direction of movement suggested? Do their bodies follow the movement or do they work against it? How does this relate to the layout of the entire page? When comics render experience through embodiment, this is often hard to perceive, but it impacts strongly on your reading.

Self-Reflexivity

Both Alison in *Fun Home* and Craig in *Blankets* are earlier versions of the narrators. There is a redoubling between the characters of the past and the authors of the present, which leads to commentaries like Bechdel's caption "heart and soul," but also to representations of the creative act itself. Alison shows herself writing and Craig shows himself in the creative and destructive process as well, as we can see in Figure 3.3 on page 64.

After his romance with Raina has come to an end, Craig sets out to destroy all memory of her. Among other things, he paints over a panel image of himself and her sitting in a tree which he had drawn on the wall of his room. The image could be an image in the comic, if it didn't show the floor boards and the paint. As Craig begins to paint over the image (and this continues over the next few pages), the page turns white, as if the images of the comic themselves were being erased. The difference between the panel image as panel image and panel

Figure 3.2 Blankets (I) © Craig Thompson. Used with Permission from TopShelf Productions.

Figure 3.2 (Cont'd) Blankets (I) © Craig Thompson. Used with Permission from TopShelf Productions.

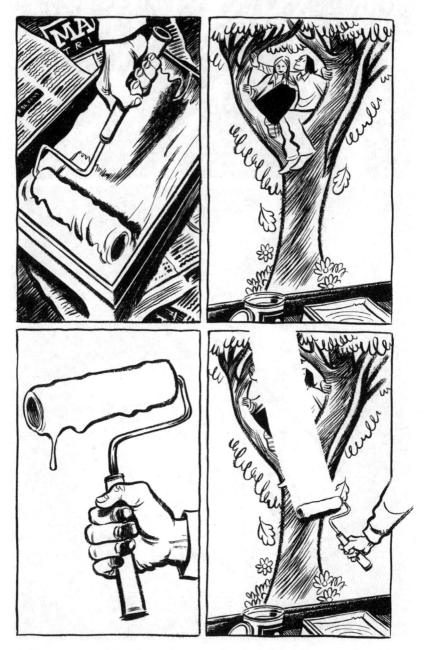

Figure 3.3 Blankets (II) © Craig Thompson. Used with Permission from TopShelf Productions.

image as representing the storyworld begins to blur. The Craig who paints in the storyworld is also the Craig who draws on the pages of the comic. Here, the inside and outside of the storyworld, the Craig of the past and the Craig of the present, merge, and both acts of painting become one.

The disembodied hand in third panel is both that of Craig in the storyworld (and a continuation of the previous two panels) and that of Craig the creator. Note that in the fourth panel, the hand reaches in from outside into the panel and that the paint erases not only the image, but also the panel frame. The panel frame is one of the unobtrusive features of the comics page. It usually goes unnoticed, but here it becomes visible. When elements of the form, such as panel frames, captions or gutters become salient, because characters jump out of the panel, because they interact with the captions (usually invisible to them) or because they take a short cut in the gutter from one panel to the another, then comics become self-reflexive. The move across the boundaries of the storyworld is called METALEPSIS. In metalepsis an element of the storyworld moves onto the metalevel of the author and readers or an element from this metalevel moves into the storyworld (for example if the hand of the author reached into the storyworld to pull Craig's ear).

In autobiographical comics, we inevitably have two temporally distinct versions of the author: his or her earlier self, which is a character in the narrative, and his or her present self, which tells and creates the story. The autobiographical pact assures readers that these two are actually the same person. Self-reflexive instances in autobiographical comics highlight the differences between the temporally distinct versions – this is the flipside to the autobiographical pact. In what follows, we will first have a closer look at these different temporal layers of the autobiographical comics and then at what its inherent self-reflexivity implies for the storytelling and the evaluation of autobiographical comics.

Time, Story, and History

Art Spiegelman's *Maus* (published in two volumes, 1986 and 1991) recounts not only the author's personal story of coming to terms with unresolved issues with his father, but also his father's own narrative of his experience of the Holocaust. Art, the main character, is comics artist Art Spiegelman who visits his father Vladek Spiegelman in order to collect material for a comic from his life's story. *Maus* thereby creates three times for its narrative: Vladek's living through the 1930s and 1940s, Vladek's telling the story to Art, and Art's reflections on what his father told him, his artistic process, and the success of the comic (especially in the second volume).

Spiegelman distinguishes Vladek's experience from his own telling of the narrative through various narrative techniques. When Vladek tells his story, you often see the Vladek of the past in the images of the panels, and the Vladek of the present narrating in the captions of the same image, quite similar to the example from *Fun Home* (Figure 3.1). When the narrative moves between the present, in which Art and Vladek have a conversation, and the past, in which we see the events unfold, Spiegelman often structures his pages in backgrounds and foregrounds (see Chapter 1). The panels representing the past events are in the foreground of the page, while the conversation between Vladek and Art in the present is shown as if in the background of these panel images.

Even though the panel images of the past use perspective to create the illusion of depth and three-dimensionality within their panel frame, in relation to the unmarked space in which the Art and Vladek of the present are situated, these images of the past seem to be flat, like the photographs, maps and drawings from the past which Spiegelman reproduces throughout the comic. The panels of Vladek's story become visualized in a way that likens them to documents from the past.

Yet not only Vladek's story but also his conversation with Art is part of the narrative in *Maus*. When Vladek and Art discuss the outcome of the Lucia episode (when Vladek gets engaged to Anja, a letter from his former lover Lucia almost prevents the marriage 2003, 25), Vladek does not want Art to record what he just told him, and the two discuss their different views on the matter. Art promises not to mention the story in his comic. Of course, the very fact that we have just read the story shows us readers that he has broken his promise. Throughout *Maus*, Spiegelman reflects not only on Vladek's story but also on his own telling of this narrative in *Maus*. Art does not tell us the story exactly as Vladek would have told it to us, and this reflection forms the third level of *Maus* in which Spiegelman addresses the artistic process itself.

Vladek's narrative is not a smooth, straightforward stream of prose, ready to be turned into a comic by Art. Vladek digresses, other characters (like Lucia) question the character he gives of himself, and he does not seem to recall what Art presents as well-known historical facts (such as the prison orchestra at Auschwitz). History is often presented as an objective account of facts about what happened in the past. Yet, as historians have been discussing for some decades now, history is always part story. By bringing events in relation to each other and by establishing causality between the facts, by highlighting certain events and ignoring others, history indeed tells a story. The historian Hayden White (1987), for example, suggests that PLOT and narrative meaning-making underlie modern history writing. This does not mean that history is fictional, or a lie, but points our attention to the narrative structures which underlie our everyday processes of meaning-making (see Chapter 2). History is our account of what happened in the past. By locating the story into a double narrative situation, of the holocaust victim who lived through the events and of the son who has to respond to this legacy, *Maus* brings the narrative nature of history to the fore, and the comic addresses the issue of authenticity.

History is not only a matter of the people who live through it, but also a matter of the people who come after it. Spiegelman represents himself in the beginning of Chapter 2 of the second volume of *Maus* as sitting on a pile of corpses. Both as the son of Holocaust survivors and as the author of a work on the Holocaust, he has to relate himself to the history he deals with. Spiegelman's endeavors to come to terms with this history can be seen in the frequent authorial comments, juxtapositions like his recounting of a story which Vladek forbids him to include in the comic, and the simultaneity of different time levels in a single panel like in the image of Spiegelman sitting on a pile of corpses.

Yet, despite the manifold narratives in *Maus*, the constant telling and retelling of history, there are also distinct gaps: Vladek has burned Anja's diaries; he is inconsistent about timelines and he claims that there was no prisoners' orchestra in Auschwitz. These gaps point towards the trauma of the Holocaust experience in Vladek's memory, and towards the trauma of Anja's suicide in both Vladek's and Art's memories. Trauma arises from instances which are not simply embarrassing or compromising like Vladek's affair with Lucia, but events which are too painful to remember and therefore cause memory lapses or the break-down of language. As Art Spiegelman tells a story about the Holocaust and two of its survivors in *Maus*, he not only highlights the problems of truthfulness in narrative, but also suggests that there are traumatic events which defy the meaning-making powers of narrative.

Box 3.2   *Identities*

Maus refers back to the funny animal cartoons, and perhaps most explicitly in Spiegelman's author portrait in the Penguin edition of the comic, in which he appears in front of an image resembling Walt Disney's Mickey Mouse. Spiegelman uses different animals to distinguish the different national groups in *Maus*: the Jews are mice, the Germans are cats, and the Poles are pigs. Spiegelman, however, complicates this simple analogy between different social groups and different animal species. When Vladek and Anja Spiegelman pretend to be non-Jewish Poles, they don pig masks. Art wonders how to draw his wife Françoise, who is French but converted to Judaism. Is she a frog (Spiegelman's animal species representing the French) or a mouse? Spiegelman addresses the idea that our identity is considered innate (you are born German, British, or French, just as animals are born a cat, a fish, or a frog), but he also begins to destabilize this assumption by showing that identities can be assumed or exchanged.

In the autobiographical comic, identity is crucially at stake. Both Thompson's *Blankets* and Bechdel's *Fun Home* present their authors in their adolescence, as they try to come to terms with their religious upbringing (in the case of *Blankets*) or their sexual orientation and their relationship to their parents (in the case of *Fun Home*). These characters are in the process of constructing their identity, which is both the way they present themselves to society and the way they think of themselves. The authors, later versions of themselves, reconstruct this identity-building by retelling the story. They choose particular moments to represent, they draw on particular images and artifacts to highlight the difference between their present self, and their earlier, yet unformed self.

Autobiographical comics represent a process of identity-building, and they reconstruct this process at the same time from a present-day point of view. They show how the character gains a sense of self, and how he or she chooses to represent him- or herself to society. Sometimes, as in Tompson's *Blankets*, they try to erase certain parts of their past, but the very fact of their telling shows that this is impossible. The identity of the autobiographical self is the sum of the outlines and drafts, the to and fro of constructing and reconstructing, which we as readers are made witness of in the narrative.

Alternative Agendas and Authenticity

Before *Maus*, the comic that was to make him famous outside the circles of comics readers, Art Spiegelman was the editor of *RAW*, an alternative comics magazine. Alternative comics, and autobiographical comics as well, follow an agenda that often puts socially marginalized issues center stage. Art Spiegelman's *Maus* engages with the Holocaust, with the guilt of the survivors, and with the weight of history that rests on the shoulders of the children. Alison Bechdel's *Fun Home* shows a young woman trying to come to terms with her relationship to her father, both being homosexual. Craig Thompson's *Blankets* deals with growing up with a disabled brother and with the impact of a religious education.

If we consider the three functions of the narrator (from Chapter 2), autobiographical comics are very playful and self-reflexive when it comes to the creative function and the transmissive function. As we have seen, *Blankets* features references to the author creating the storyworld, and both *Fun Home* and *Maus* are self-reflexive about how their narrators communicate their narrative. However, they stress the function of testifying to the authenticity of the tale. Art Spiegelman for example suggested in a letter to the editor of the *New York Times Book Review* (29 December 1991) that *Maus* should be classed as "non-fiction/mice." Alison Bechdel posed and took pictures of herself for every panel she drew for *Fun Home*. Each of these comics insists on the authenticity of the individual experience.

On the other hand, these comics comment on the storytelling process itself, highlighting its gaps, inconsistencies and detours, as does for example Spiegelman in *Maus*. Sitting in the car with his wife Françoise, Art comments that "in real life you'd never have let me talk this long without interrupting" (2003, 176). Spiegelman suggests that the requirements of storytelling already distort a rendition of the events as they actually took place. However, in the very act of highlighting this problem, he is honest with his readers and authentic as an author. He can never represent reality one to one in his comic, but on the other hand, such transparency, such a seemingly unproblematic immersion, is the hallmark of fiction. By outlining and reflecting on the problems in telling a story, its rhetoric and the maneuvers to make the events tellable in the first place, autobiographical comics step closer to a realism of storytelling.

The borders of authenticity are carefully policed. Craig Thompson's *Blankets*, for example, has been described as a "vulgarization" of autobiographical comics because it tells a "feel-good romance, playing the heart-strings of readers" (Menu 2005, 39).[1] Jean-Christophe Menu, the former director of the French alternative comics publisher L'Association, claims that *Blankets* is a comic produced by an accomplished draughtsman but ultimately lacks in authenticity. Menu's assessment suggests that authenticity and immersive appeal, which Thompson achieves partly through his gorgeous drawing style and partly through his shrewd use of embodiment, are two fundamentally different things. What's more, Menu constructs a hierarchy between authenticity and immersive appeal which assigns *Blankets* to the bottom. Of course, Menu writes in the context of French comics publishing; yet this account of *Blankets* shows the importance which the genre assigns to authenticity, understood as giving access "raw" experience. As the autobiographical comics have become perhaps the most respected genre in comics today, it also points towards an elitist distinction emerging which takes autobiographical comics far away from their underground origins.

Note

1   The original French reads "romance pleine de bons sentiments et d'effets violonneux"; the translation is mine. My thanks to Ann Miller for pointing out Menu's response to *Blankets* to me.

Recommended Reading

Baetens, Jan. 2001. "Revealing Traces: A New Theory of Graphic Enunciation." In *The Language of Comics: Words and Image*, edited by Robin Varnum and Christina Gibbons, 145–55. Jackson: University Press of Mississippi.
Lejeune, Philippe. 1989. *On Autobiography*. Trans. Paul Eakin. Minneapolis: University of Minnesota Press.

Two key theoretical texts: Baetens reconsiders Marion's (1993) account of graphiation in English.

Hatfield, Charles. 2005. *Alternative Comics: An Emerging Literature*. Jackson: University Press of Mississippi.
Witek, Joseph. 1986. *Comic Books as History: The Narrative Art of Jack Jackson, Art Spiegelman and Harvey Pekar*. Jackson: University Press of Mississippi.
Rosenkranz, Patrick. 2008. *Rebel Visions: The Underground Comix Revolution 1963–75*. Seattle: Fantagraphics.
Beaty, Bart. 2007. *Unpopular Culture: Transforming the European Comic Book in the 1990s*. Toronto: University of Toronto Press.

Hatfield's book gives perhaps the most comprehensive account of alternative comics, from their underground roots to today. Witek outlines the connections between EC Comics and the underground comics, while Rosenkranz offers an overview on the entire period. Beaty focuses on European comics, but his account of autobiography and authenticity is important for English-language comics as well.

Park, Hye Su. 2011. "Art Spiegelman's *Maus*: A Survivor's Tale: A Bibliographic Essay." *Shofar*, 29.2: 319–42.

Whitlock, Gillian and Anna Poletti, eds. Autographics. Special issue of *Biography*, 31.1.

McGlothlin, Erin. 2003. "No Time Like the Present: Narrative and Time in Art Spiegelman's *Maus*." *Narrative*, 11: 177–98.

Chute, Hillary. 2010. *Graphic Women: Life Narrative and Contemporary Comics*. New York: Columbia University Press.

Warhol, Robyn. 2011. "The Space Between: A Narrative Approach to Alison Bechdel's *Fun Home*." *College Literature*, 38.3: 1–20.

Many articles have been published on autobiographical comics and their storytelling in general, and on *Maus* in particular. Park's bibliographical essay gives you a place to start when you want to know what has been written on *Maus*. The special issue of the journal *Biography* presents literary analyses of a number of autobiographical comics. McGlothlin investigates the three layers of time in the narrative in *Maus*, Chute gives an overview on female authors of autobiographical comics, while Warhol focuses on the different levels of narration in *Fun Home*.

References

Lejeune, Philippe. 1989. *On Autobiography*. Trans. Paul Eakin. Minneapolis: University of Minnesota Press.

Marion, Philippe. 1993. *Traces en Cases: Travail graphique, figuration narrative et participation du lecture*. Louvain-la-Neuve: Academia.

Menu, Jean-Christophe. 2005. *Plates-bandes*. Paris: L'Association.

Spiegelman, Art. 1991. "A Problem of Taxonomy." *New York Times* (29 December). Online. Last Accessed 27 October 2012. http://www.nytimes.com/1991/12/29/books/l-a-problem-of-taxonomy-37092.html

White, Hayden. 1987. *The Content of Form: Narrative Discourse and Historical Representation*. Baltimore: Johns Hopkins University Press.

Comics Discussed

Bechdel, Alison. 2006. *Fun Home: A Family Tragicomic*. London: Jonathan Cape.

Spiegelman, Art. 2003. *The Complete Maus*. London: Penguin.

Thompson, Craig. 2011. *Blankets: A Graphic Novel*. Portland: TopShelf.

Class Activity 3: The Autobiographical Pact

Get together in small groups, with one half of the group assuming the role of the author of an autobiography and the other half of the group assuming the role of the reader of an autobiography, and renegotiate the autobiographical pact. What can an author promise his reader in terms of honesty and authenticity? What freedoms does she need to reserve for herself? What can a reader demand from her author in this genre? If time allows, put the contract you arrive at down in writing.

Writing Assignment 3

Take a page from *Maus*, *Fun Home* or *Blankets*. Track the clues on the page which refer to the author in the present, and those who refers to the author in the past. Are the narrator, the focalizer or the observer marked on the page? Does the page feature any self-reflexive elements? How would you describe the graphiation (lines, contours, and colors)? Write 300–500 words.

Essay Question 3

Realism in Autography
Craig Thompson's *Blankets*, even though it is an autobiographical comic, presents several instances in which the narrative breaks with a strictly realist agenda. In their game play, Craig and his brother turn into the beasts they impersonate. Craig finds himself in the midst of a biblical narrative and imagines a picture of Jesus responding to his actions. Consider these and other departures from realism in *Blankets*: what function(s) do they have in Thompson's narrative?

Do such non-realist elements in autobiographical comics betray the autobiographical pact? Do they break with the authenticity required of narratives in the genre? Where do they place autobiography on the scale between fiction and non-fiction?

4

Novels and Graphic Novels: Adaptations

Comics have a distinct and recognizable way of telling a story in images, words, and sequence which is distinct from novels or films. In this chapter, we will consider how the process of transporting a story from one medium to another works and how such adaptation shapes the narrative itself, focusing in particular on adaptations of novels in comics. Key issues will be what particular media can and cannot do (so-called "media affordances"), the question of how an adaptation can be "true" to the original, and how comics recreate specific literary strategies, such as COGNITIVE COMPLEXITY and DEFAMILIARIZATION.

Box 4.1   *Comics Convergence Culture*

Henry Jenkins coined the term "convergence culture" in order to describe how one story extends into many different media, from film to novels, comics and video games, how different media industries cooperate in this process and how audiences migrate between different media. Transmedia storytelling, the aspect of convergence culture which I am most interested in here, is discussed by Jenkins (2006) for such cultural phenomena as *The Matrix*, *Star Wars*, and *Harry Potter*. Comics and the comics industry are also heavily invested in transmedia storytelling (with a particular emphasis on the participatory culture around them). From its very beginning, the medium has

---

Studying Comics and Graphic Novels, First Edition. Karin Kukkonen.
© 2013 John Wiley & Sons, Ltd. Published 2013 by John Wiley & Sons, Ltd.

exported its stories into other media. This has been discussed for the British character Ally Sloper from the beginning of the twentieth century (see Sabin 2003), and it is perhaps most strikingly noticeable for Superman, whose comic book run started in 1938 and who had a film series, a radio show, and a range of toys before the end of the 1940s. The storytelling in comics often emerges through an intermedial web, in which parts of the common story have been developed in different installments and in different media.

Superman is a case in point for the intermedial web around comics and for how the affordances of different media contribute to the development of a character in transmedia storytelling. The Superman of the early comics, for example, could jump but not fly. This looked good on the images of a comic book, which display only the "pregnant moment," but much less dignified on film. So when the first Superman (short) films were shot, the hero gained the ability to fly. When Superman was adapted for radio, producers were faced with the problem that they could not show what the hero was doing, that he would not be talking much himself while fighting, and that a lengthy narrator's discourse would slow down the action. They therefore gave a larger role to the young photographer Jimmy Olsen, who would excitedly relate and comment on what was happening (see Fuchs and Reitberger 1972, 163). Later on, Jimmy Olsen would become a frequently-featured character in the comics with his own series *Superman's Pal Jimmy Olsen*. As *Superman* demonstrates, transmedia storytelling unfolds in many different media and converges towards a larger story universe. These media, however, are not simply transparent channels for the story to flow through. On the contrary, their particular features and their affordances change and adapt what they tell continually.

Transporting Stories

With the intertextual web of transmedial storytelling, an adaptation constitutes one mode of connection which transports a story and its characters from one medium to another. A closer focus on this transporting process reveals the difficulties in moving between media. A comics version of Emily Brontë's *Wuthering Heights* and a novel version can obviously not be the same, because of media differences between novels and comics. How do these differences between media affect the way in which the story is told? Does this mean that one medium is generally better than another?

In the introduction to this book, we have defined comics as a medium in three respects: a medium is a channel of communication, a set of technologies, and a social context of institutions, such as publishing houses and infrastructures of distribution. In this chapter, I will concentrate on the medium as a channel of communication and storytelling, even though the social context of institutions plays an important role for deciding what gets adapted and how much cultural prestige it gathers (see Chapter 5). A medium communicates through a number of modes, which for comics are the visual, the verbal, and the sequential. Comics are therefore a "multimodal medium." Each mode favors particular ways of communicating. In other words, there are certain things modes and their combination in a medium do well and certain things they do poorly. Some of these features we have already discussed through Lessing's distinction between the "art of time" and the "art of space" (Chapter 1) and through the issue of telling and showing in images and words (Chapter 2).These capabilities and limitations are called "media affordances."

Media Affordances and Adaptation Strategies

In adapting novels, comics have to translate narrative strategies from the written word into images, words, and sequence. They need to deal with verbal ambiguity, the differences between descriptions in words and images, the pacing and perspectives of narration when subject to panel divisions, and (sometimes) the restricted length of the comic-book format.

Comics employ images (rather than words) to represent the characters and settings, and they therefore often have to be more specific than novels are about the way an element looks in the storyworld. In *Wuthering Heights*, for example, the main character Heathcliff is described as a "dark-skinned gypsy in aspect," but also as simply "dirty," and the housekeeper suggests that he is not a "black." The question of Heathcliff's precise looks and ethnic origin keeps shifting in the novel. In the *Classics Illustrated* version (Figure 4.1), Heathcliff is a dark-haired romantic hero. In R. Sikoryak's *Masterpiece* version (Figure 4.2), he is of a decidedly dark skin color. Unlike a novel, a comic will find it difficult to remain ambiguous about a character's look or to state a negative, such as "Heathcliff was not black."

A novel can take more time in unfolding its descriptions, whereas the images in comics usually present the scene at a single glance. Brontë's novel details

Figure 4.1 *Wuthering Heights* in the Classics Illustrated Version. Copyright © 2012 by First Classics, Inc. All rights reserved. Used by permission of Jack Lake Productions Inc.

Figure 4.1 (Cont'd) *Wuthering Heights* in the Classics Illustrated Version.
Copyright © 2012 by First Classics, Inc. All rights reserved. Used by permission of
Jack Lake Productions Inc.

Figure 4.2 *Wuthering Heights* in R. Sikoryak's Version. From *Masterpiece Comics* (Drawn and Quarterly 2009) Copyright 2009 R. Sikoryak.

Heathcliff's first impressions when he and Cathy spy on the Lintons in their living room thus: "a splendid place carpeted with crimson, and crimson-covered chairs and tables, and a pure white ceiling bordered by gold, a shower of glass drops hanging by silver chains from the centre, and shimmering with little soft tapers" (2010, 50). Whereas Brontë's novel slowly moves Heathcliff's perception from the splendor of the Linton's place to the fight of its denizens over the dog, in both comics versions the fight immediately grabs readers' attention when they get a view of the living room. The *Classics Illustrated* version indicates the juxtaposition between the splendid and civilized house and the fight by placing a lamp and book on the polished table on the left, preceding the fight in the general reading direction of the image. In both comics, however, the dog forms the peak of the triangle of the gazes of participants and the fight informs readers' first impression of the living room, because the acting characters command more attention than the interior. Lessing's notion of the "pregnant moment" (see Chapter 1) can be particularly helpful when considering how comics and novels set their scene.

Because comics employ words and images, they have to strike a balance between how much of the original words of the novel they keep and how much they represent in images. They also have to decide how to represent changing perspectives in narration. The *Classics Illustrated* version, for example, alternates between the (grouped) focalization of Heathcliff and Cathy and that of the Lintons on the second page. The first panel shows the two contemplating what they see, the second panel reveals that they are seen, in turn, by the Lintons. The third panel then shows the intensity of the struggle against the dog in a round panel focusing on Heathcliff and Cathy, whereas the fourth panel shows them as silhouettes being seen by a member of the Linton household. The mirroring of Heathcliff and Cathy's figures from the round panel to the silhouette, and the frequent changes of perspective, underscore the dramatic pacing of the scene in the visual mode.

The *Classics Illustrated* version uses a heterodiegetic narrator throughout in the captions. The *Masterpiece* version keeps the embedded homodiegetic narratives of the housekeeper (in the caption of the first panel) and of Heathcliff himself (in captions from the second panel onwards). The images of his recollection are presented as if in a thought bubble, and the focalization is consistently with Heathcliff. In the third panel, for example, he is much more prominent than in the corresponding image of the *Classics Illustrated* version. The dramatic tension here revolves around his separation from Cathy. Unlike the *Classics Illustrated* version, their attention is often divided and their gazes are directed in different ways. The diagonal compositions of the two final panels of the page each present Heathcliff on a vector leading away from Cathy. Both versions make a choice as to where the dynamic center of the scene in the novel is located, and different decisions in terms of narration, focalization, and composition ensue on the comics page.

Comics adaptations tend to condense the stories of novels, especially if they are in the classic comic book format. The novel *Wuthering Heights* is 356 pages long (in the edition I use). The *Classics Illustrated* version is forty-five pages long, and the *Masterpiece* version only fifteen pages. To some extent, this shortening is occasioned by the use of images representing "pregnant moments" and by reducing the narrative discourse to dialogue elements. However, generally, the pacing of the plot is faster in these shorter versions, too, and side plots and frame narratives are often dropped.

What comics have in common with novels is the fact that they are printed on paper and bound into a book-format publication. Unlike film, this allows readers to skim the pages and to jump back and forth between chapters if they choose to do so. Readers can also judge more conveniently how far into the novel or the comic they are in their reading and how long the story will last still. Unlike novels, whose pagination will change from edition to edition, comics have a fixed-page layout which will remain the same in any edition. As we have seen before, the page layout in comics is often meaningful for grouping events, not unlike a chapter boundary in a novel.

The media affordances of comics overlap in some respects with those of the novel, but their differences are salient and lead to significant changes when stories are transported from novels into comics. When considering adaptations, a good starting point is to trace the changes between the different versions back to the media affordances of novels and comics.

Fidelity in Adaptation

Adaptations are sometimes evaluated in terms of their FIDELITY, of how "true" to the original text they are. But what does that mean exactly? Which of the two *Wuthering Heights* versions has the greater degree of fidelity? Key criteria of fidelity would be setting the graphic novel in the period when the novel takes place (around 1800), and keeping the characters and events from the novel, together with as much of the dialogue as possible. Yet, in order to compress the events of the novel into the pages of the comic book, the narrative has been modified in both comics versions: Emily Brontë's novel famously begins with the new tenant at Thrushcross Grange, Mr. Lockwood, encountering Heathcliff and staying for a nightmare-ridden night at Wuthering Heights, before he learns about the events from the housekeeper Mrs. Dean. Both the *Classics Illustrated* and the *Masterpiece* version do without this frame story. In the *Masterpiece* version, Heathcliff's marriage to Isabel Linton and their son's marriage to Catherine Linton have also been cut, and the narrative deals only with the first generation of characters. Still, both comics versions keep some of the dialogue from the novel, as for example "Keep fast, Skulker" in the *Masterpiece* version, or the dialogue between Cathy and Heathcliff in the second panel of the *Classics Illustrated* version, which is taken straight from the novel.

Comics in the *Classics Illustrated* series often include dialogue and salient phrases from their originals, which underlines the emphasis the series places on fidelity in adaptation. In other respects, the *Classics Illustrated* version moves away from the novel. By the looks of the characters, it sets its story slightly later than Brontë's novel. In fact, its period setting is that of the highly successful 1938 film version by William Wyler (see Jones 2011), demonstrating the degree to which adaptations are part of transmedial storytelling.

Creators might indeed decide to foreground their own interpretation by changing details of the setting, the appearance of the characters or the way they communicate. This approach considers an adaptation as a translation of the classic, or perhaps even as a challenge to the classic and our assumptions about it, rather than as a reproduction in a different medium. An adaptation which translates a classic for new audience places it into a new context and thereby suggests new perspectives on a well-known text. The *Masterpiece* version of *Wuthering Heights*, for example, positions itself as a "translation" of this kind, even though it employs a period setting in both images and language. R. Sikoryak's *The Crypt of Brontë* sets Emily Brontë's *Wuthering Heights* in the genre of the EC horror comic.

As you can see from the title page of the comic (Figure 4.3), the *Masterpiece* version alludes to the EC title "The Crypt of Horror" and the usual presentation of the narrators of EC comics. EC comics, a publisher of popular and exploitative horror comics, censored and reviled in their time, seems to be very different from Brontë's Victorian novel, which is celebrated by critics and scholars and read in schools.

In fact, however, the *Masterpiece* version's choice of EC comics as a context for its adaptation connects to Brontë's *Wuthering Heights* rather well. They both belong to the same genre, the Gothic or horror genre. Wuthering Heights is "swarming with ghosts and goblins" as the narrator Lockwood puts it (2010, 28), and Heathcliff is more than once likened to the devil in the novel. At the end of the *Masterpiece* comic, Heathcliff tells Mrs. Dean that he had opened Cathy's coffin to be close to her. We see him embracing the corpse. This is an instance which the *Classics Illustrated* version tactfully omits; in Brontë's novel, there are a series of approximations to this event, when Heathcliff recounts how Catherine's

Figure 4.3   The Heights! From *Masterpiece Comics* (Drawn and Quarterly 2009) Copyright 2009 R. Sikoryak.

coffin accidentally opens when digging Linton's grave, how he opened up her grave again, and how he felt she was close by in this moment (2010, 304–5).

Another point of contact between Brontë's novel and the EC comic tradition is their extensive use of personalized narrators. Even though the *Masterpiece*

Comics version does not make use of the frame story around Heathcliff's tenant Mr. Lockwood, it frequently refers to Mrs. Dean's narrative, casting her as "the House Keeper" in analogy with EC comics' the Crypt Keeper, and at the end of her narrative she refers readers back to the Lockwood narrative: "I suppose The Tenant will have his own story for you." The multiple narrative frames of the Brontë novel are evoked, if not enacted, in the *Masterpiece Comics* version. In this adaptation, EC comics serves as a new context of relevance for Brontë's novel, updating its genre in a more contemporary frame and casting new light on its generic allegiances.

If the *Classics Illustrated*'s version stresses fidelity in adaptation and moves the comic closer to the high-culture association of Brontë's novel, the *Masterpiece* version seems to stress translation and move towards the popular tradition of comics as a medium (see the next chapter for more details on the value hierarchy between high culture and popular culture). However, there are more connections between the *Classics Illustrated* and the *Masterpiece* version than this simple dichotomy along the lines of "fidelity" suggests. Both EC comics and Gilberton, the publisher of *Classics Illustrated* at the time, opted out from the self-censorship of the comics industry in the 1950s (more on this in the next chapter), and Gilberton in fact hired many EC artists for *Classics Illustrated* after the demise of its horror comics lines (see Jones 2011, 165). *Classics Illustrated* stresses fidelity to its originals and its pedagogic mission, yet it is also part of a larger context of media storytelling. *Masterpiece* positions itself clearly as a translation yet it also works as a commentary on *Wuthering Heights*'s relation to the horror genre. The fidelity question might offer a convenient sorting mechanism for adaptations but, ultimately, the cross-connections that unfold between different versions are of far greater interest to the study of comics.

Box 4.2   Classics Illustrated

Classics Illustrated is the name of a comic book series that specializes in adaptations of literary classics in the comics medium. The series was started as "Classic Comics" in 1941 by Albert Kantner for the US market with an adaptation of Alexandre Dumas' *The Three Musketeers*. Adaptations of historical adventure novels, like Sir Walter Scott's *Ivanhoe* or James Fenimore Cooper's *The Last of the Mohicans*, soon followed. After a very successful run in the 1940s and 1950s, the publication of new titles stopped in 1962, and the entire production of

Classics Illustrated came to a halt in 1971. The *Classics Illustrated* label survives, and the old comics are still available in new editions. *Classics Illustrated* is the best-known publisher of comics adaptations, but other comics publishers have launched their own lines for adaptations of the classics, too. In pedagogical adaptations of literary classics, the comics are designed to be easier to read than the novel in order to prepare students for reading the actual classic.

If you consider the list of well over a hundred classic novels which were adapted for the *Classics Illustrated* comic books, you will notice that most of these novels, even though they carry the status of "classics" by now, were actually popular reading material at the time of their publication. Dumas' *The Three Musketeers* (*Classics Illustrated* #1) was serialized in a newspaper between March and July 1844. Daniel Defoe's *Robinson Crusoe* (*Classics Illustrated* #10) provided a highly popular narrative of a castaway, his religious conversion and travels to exotic places. Wilkie Collins's *The Moonstone* (*Classics Illustrated* #30) is an example of the Victorian sensationalist novel, and Jules Verne's *Michael Strogoff* (*Classics Illustrated* #28) belongs to the nineteenth-century novel of adventures. There are certainly exceptions to this tendency, but *Classics Illustrated* mostly adapted novels that contained action-based plots and were classics precisely because of their popular success. They prized fidelity to the original by keeping the narrative in as complete a form as possible and by including salient lines from the novels into the dialogue. At the end of the comic book, they would characteristically suggest to readers to go on to read the original classic novel.

Box 4.3   *The Graphic Novel*

The graphic novel is a publication format for comics which rose to prominence in the 1990s. It generally refers to a comic which is published in its entirety, as opposed to serialized comic books which will later be collected into trade paperbacks. The term gained currency with Will Eisner's *A Contract With God*, which Eisner described as a "graphic novel." *A Contract With God* features a set of interwoven short stories that are published in their entirety as a graphic novel (and not as a set of comic books). However, since the success of Eisner's term and the beginning of the cultural reevaluation of comics at the end of the twentieth century, many comics will be sold under the label "graphic novel" even if they are technically trade paperbacks. Indeed, most of the comics distinguished by criticism today, like *Watchmen* or Art Spiegelman's *Maus*, were originally published in serial form.

The component "novel" in the term "graphic novel" connects comics explicitly to the larger category of literature. "Literature" is often understood as denoting an example of high culture. When comics came increasingly to be considered as valuable cultural products, the connection to literature was a welcome one, and publishers and distributors of comics therefore quickly adopted the term "graphic novel." In parallel with the cultural valorization of comics that is exemplified by the rise of the term "graphic novel," comics publishers have also started adopting the production modes of high culture by bringing out special editions of their most successful comics in an expensive hardback format, by keeping titles available in trade paperbacks and by collecting and republishing old stories in archive editions. Aesthetic, cultural, and commercial issues are closely entwined in the format of the "graphic novel."

Literary Complexity

Comics are generally considered to be less "literary" than novels: they seem to be less ambiguous, they seem to represent less cognitive complexity, and they seem to offer a more straight-forward and less perplexing reading experience. But comics can also leave readers to draw their own conclusions, display a plurality of perspectives, and reflect on the features of their form. In this section and the next, we will see how comics put these capacities for literary complexity to work in adapting literary works.

We have noted with regard to Heathcliff's looks that comics find it generally much harder than written texts to be non-specific. Language can easily leave the most important things unrepresented. Consider for example the marriage proposal of Edward Ferrars to Elinor Dashwood in Jane Austen's *Sense and Sensibility*:

His errand at Barton, in fact, was a simple one. It was only to ask Elinor to marry him; – and considering that he was not altogether inexperienced in such a question, it might be strange that he should feel so uncomfortable in the present case as he really did, so much in need of encouragement and fresh air.

How soon he had walked himself into the proper resolution, however, how soon an opportunity of exercising it occurred, in what manner he expressed himself, and how he was received, need not be particularly told. This only need be said; – that when they all sat down to table at four o'clock, three hours after his arrival, he had secured his lady, engaged her mother's consent, and was not only in the rapturous profession of the lover, but in the reality of reason and truth, one of the happiest of men. (2006, 386)

Austen studiously avoids being specific about one of the events her entire novel hinges upon. What exactly happens and when, as she puts it, "need not be particularly told." Austen does not locate the moment of the proposal in the flow of events, and she certainly does not give any details about it. She only tells readers that it was before "they all sat down to table at four o'clock." How can a comic adapt this scene?

In the comics version, Edward proposes to Elinor in the middle panel of the page. At first glance, this seems to overspecify the event which Austen leaves so undefined. However, we are not actually witnessing the proposal here either. Edward tells Elinor that his "errand" is to propose to her, but he takes her on a walk away from the watchful eyes of her family, just like Austen removes the proposal scene from her readers' knowledge. The panel in which he mentions the proposal has no panel frame. It spills behind the other panels, and its white background is not marked by the details of the room they stand in. Through these devices, the comic takes away specificity in time and space, just as Austen does in her novel. The emotional tension which underlies the scene is captured in the close up of Edward and Elinor, being drawn to each other but with the barrier of the (as of yet) unspoken proposal poised between them in the speech bubbles.

In the comics version, Edward, and not the narrator, expresses his uneasiness about this situation to Elinor. Here, the characters communicate their purposes and feelings in dialogue (and to each other). In the novel version, the narrator communicates the purposes and feelings of the characters to the reader. The comic seems to take away one level of embedding, one level of what Lisa Zunshine (2011) calls "socio-cognitive complexity," in relation to the novel. In the novel, we have the narrator ironically reflecting on Edward, who has already

Figure 4.4 Sense and Sensibility (I). *Source*: from *Sense and Sensibilities* 2010. TM and © 2013 Marvel and Subs.

proposed once before, being nervous, and readers are not certain whether Edward is aware of the irony. The level of the narrator and the level of the character are distinct and contribute to our experience of cognitive complexity. In the comic, Edward expresses his nervousness himself. This seems to take away the level of the narrator, and the cognitive complexity occasioned by it, but in fact, considering the shocked expression on his face, readers cannot be sure whether Edward is aware of the irony as he utters it. Through the juxtaposition of the verbal and visual mode, Edward's discourse and his facial expression, placed there as clues by the narrator, the discrepancy between the comics narrator's knowledge as communicated to the reader and the character's own knowledge comes back in, and with it cognitive complexity.

Comics find it more difficult than the novel does to render in language layers of the knowledge different characters have about each other, but they are quite capable of producing cognitive complexity through other means.

When earlier in the novel, Colonel Brandon suggests to Elinor that he will give a parish living to Edward, Mrs. Jennings overhears the conversation and conjectures that Colonel Brandon is proposing to Elinor on the strength of Elinor's reaction and some elements of dialogue she overhears. Austen introduces cognitive complexity here to set up a misunderstanding that will only be resolved later on: (1) the narrator communicates that (2) Mrs. Jennings thinks (3) that Colonel Brandon proposes to Elinor. The comic similarly presents three basic levels: the interaction between Colonel Brandon and Elinor, Mrs. Jennings' eavesdropping, and the ironic perspective of the narrator. Indeed, we can identify more levels at different points in the scene, for example, when Mrs. Jennings positions herself as listening to Marianne so that Elinor, the Colonel and Marianne would not be suspicious of her curiosity. Mrs. Jennings does not want anyone else to know that she wants to know and the levels of cognitive complexity start proliferating.

In the comic, the interaction between Colonel Brandon and Elinor takes place in the background of the second panel, and in the inserted panels of the third panel. Mrs. Jennings looks ostentatiously at the exchange in both panels, and assumes that, by eavesdropping, getting knowledge about the other two characters, she gains access to a higher level of cognitive complexity. Mrs. Jennings' straining to move to a higher level of knowledge is represented in the third panel, where the superimposed panels with Elinor and Colonel Brandon's exchange are so arranged that it seems Mrs. Jennings is trying to peer into them. This arrangement of the panels, together with Mrs. Jennings' attempt to eavesdrop and her statement in the fourth panel

Figure 4.5 Sense and Sensibility (II) 2010. TM and © 2013 Marvel and Subs.

that "try as I might" she "could not help overhearing" the conversation, creates the third, ironic level of the narrator. At the same time, Mrs. Jennings' turning her head away while trying to peek and the careful distance she keeps from the couple reflect the extra levels of cognitive complexity that we also find in Austen's novel.

We began this chapter by considering the different affordances of comics and novels. Some of these affordances, like the novel's capacity to avoid being specific and to render layers of cognitive complexity, are connected to the notion of "literariness" and seem to preclude successful adaptations of novels like Jane Austen's which thrive on exactly these affordances of the written word. Comics, however, can work around these limitations, and present undefined panels, removed from time and space, or suggest ironic reflections on the characters' misconceptions.

The Page Revisited

Despite their differences in terms of the media affordances of images and words, both comics and novels are printed and bound in book-like publications. And, even though for most novels the page layout is not fixed, there are a few novels that draw attention to the unity of the page, their typography, and the fact that they are bound printed matter with pages to turn. A classic example for this approach is Laurence Sterne's novel *Tristram Shandy* (1761–7). In *Tristram Shandy*, readers encounter blacked-out pages to mourn Yorick, the parson. Pages are left empty so that readers can draw their own picture of widow Wadman, "as like your mistress as you can – as unlike your wife as your conscience will let you" (2009, 376). The progress of the plot of *Tristram Shandy*, and its digressions, is represented in a series of lines (see Figure 4.6):

The Life and Opinions of Tristram Shandy, Gentleman purports to be an auto-biographical account of Tristram Shandy, who serves as the narrator of the novel. However, readers do not reach Tristram's birth until volume three (of the nine-volume novel). The frequent digressions and the rambling narrative progress of *Tristram Shandy* give readers both a rich sense of life in the Shandy family and of Tristram's own fictional mind. And, despite these digressions, Tristram's energetic narrative voice carries readers along.

In the comics adaptation of *Tristram Shandy*, Martin Rowson makes use of the properties of the comics page in order to capture in particular the drive of Tristram's narration (see Figure 4.7; page over).

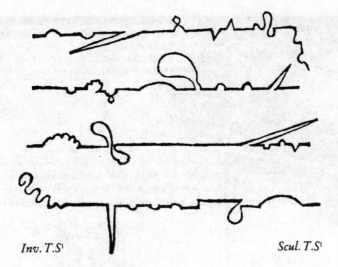

Inv. T.S¹   *Scul. T.S¹*

Figure 4.6 From Sterne's *Tristram Shandy.*

In Rowson's comic, the narrator Tristram enters the frame riding a rocket at the top left of the first panel. After an excursion to the celestial bodies, and their influence on his life, he enters the sphere of the main narrative again. Following the crash landing of the rocket, Tristram takes three characters, who work as stand-ins for the actual readers, along with him across the page until he shoves them out of the panel frame in the last panel. Several processes are at work here: (i) the route across the page is mapped on the reader's progression through the narrative; (ii) the way the narrator guides and teases the reader is represented in the images; and (iii) the clear direction the narrative should take looms in the background of the narrator's antics. Let's discuss each of these issues in turn.

First, the path of Tristram and his readers across the page is the same as the path which the actual readers' gaze takes across the page. The story as a movement through the space and time of the storyworld is represented as the movement through the space of the page and the time it takes to read it. The page from the *Tristram Shandy* comic presents an embodied correlate to readers' progress through the story, as it maps it on to the characters' progress across the page. The particularities of this "progress" are represented in the encounter between Tristram and his readers. Tristram on the page here quotes

Figure 4.7 Rowson's *Tristram Shandy*. © Martin Rowson.

directly from the narrative discourse of the novel (2009, 10–11), and the images show how Tristram's discourse treats the readers: it coaxes them through suggesting "familiarity" and "friendship" in the third panel, it makes them stand still as it attaches the nose rings, and it pulls and pushes them along ruthlessly. The comic represents in the images what the narrator Tristram does to readers in his narrative. In this passage in the novel, the process is not spelled out, but Tristram's frequent addresses to the readers and his explanations as to his narrative strategies throughout Sterne's novel offer the template for this representation in the comic. The narrator in comics is often invisible, but here, as in Sterne's novel, he comes to the fore and makes his work transparent. The digressive nature of Tristram's narrative is highlighted by the sign post to "Ye Narrative" which stands in the background, as Tristram guides his readers towards it and then away from it. Like the plot lines in the *Tristram Shandy* novel (Figure 4.6), which are not straight lines but which visualize the digressions of Tristram, the signpost suggests a narrative norm from which Tristram deviates.

Viktor Shklovsky famously called Sterne's *Tristram Shandy* "the most typical novel in world literature" (1965, 57) because (through its self-reflexivity) it highlights the dynamics of the novel as such. The comic *Tristram Shandy* makes visible the dynamics of the plot in the interaction between the signposts of "ye narrative" and the extensions and contractions between story and discourse in Tristram's encounter with the readers, as he drags them across the page. For Shklovsky, the novel *Tristram Shandy* defamiliarizes the novel form, because it brings its constituent elements and dynamics to the fore. Rowson's comic version of *Tristram Shandy* does something similar, as it highlights the workings of the comic's narrative and its movement across time and space on the page. Rowson extends this to the famous black page in *Tristram Shandy*: in his comic, Tristram and the readers literally crash against the black monolith of the page, much as readers of the novel come to a halt in the flow of reading at this point. The plot lines themselves (Figure 4.6) feature as a race course through which Tristram rushes his readers. On almost every page of the comic, these plot lines from the novel have become paths along which Tristram drags the readers across the page. Rowson works through several strategies of mise en page and embodying readers, all of which serve to defamiliarize the reading process of the comic, much as the constant pointers towards the narrative discourse in Sterne's *Tristram Shandy* defamiliarizes the dynamics of the novel.

* * *

Comics as a medium are different from the novel. They work through images and words in sequence, and they rely on the page layout to create meaningful units of their narrative matter. Transporting a narrative from a novel into a comic, or graphic novel, therefore constitutes an adaptation. In adaptations, questions of fidelity and media affordances have to be considered. However, through their own affordances and narrative strategies, comics can reproduce elements which are traditionally considered "literary" and connected to the novel, such as the cognitive complexity of a Jane Austen novel or the self-reflexivity and defamiliarization of *Tristram Shandy*.

Recommended Reading

Stam, Robert. 2005. "Introduction: The Theory and Practice of Film Adaptation." In *Literature and Film: A Guide to the Theory and Practice of Film Adaptation*, edited by Robert Stam and Alessandra Raegno, 1–52. Oxford: Blackwell.
McFarlane, Brian. 1996. *Novel to Film: An Introduction to the Theory of Adaptation*. Oxford: Clarendon.

As of this writing, I am not aware of any book devoted specifically to comics adaptations of novels. The debate around film adaptations of novels, as outlined in Stam and McFarlane, however, offers a useful overview of issues relevant for comics adaptations as well.

Jenkins, Henry, 2006. *Convergence Culture: Where Old and New Media Collide*. New York: New York University Press.
Kress, Gunther and Theo van Leuven. 2001. *Multimodal Discourse: The Modes and Media of Contemporary Communication*. London: Arnold.
Sabin, Roger. 2003. "Ally Sloper: The First Comics Superstar?" *Image and Narrative*, 7. Last accessed: October 15, 2012. http://www.imageandnarrative.be/inarchive/graphicnovel/rogersabin.htm (09 April 2013)

Both the books by Jenkins and Kress and van Leuven consider the different possible connections between media: Jenkins focuses on convergence culture, which brings different media together in a cultural and narrative context; Kress and van Leuven focus on multi-modality, the interactions of different modes within a single medium. Sabin gives an example of transmedial storytelling at the turn of the twentieth century.

Versaci, Rocco. 2007. *This Book Contains Graphic Language: Comics as Literature*. London: Continuum. Ch.6 "Illustrating the Classics: Comic Books vs. 'Real' Literature."
Jones, William B. Jr. 2011. *Classics Illustrated: A Cultural History*. 2nd edition. Jefferson, NC: McFarland.

Zunshine, Lisa. 2011. "What to Expect When You Pick Up A Graphic Novel" *SubStance*, 40.1: 114–34.

Shklovsky, Viktor. 1965. "Art as Technique" and "Sterne's *Tristram Shandy*: Stylistic Commentary." In *Russian Formalist Criticism: Four Essays*, 3–24 and 25–57. Lincoln: University of Nebraska Press.

Jones tells a detailed history of the *Classics Illustrated* series, whereas Versacci reflects on the *Classics Illustrated* series and its cultural impact. Zunshine investigates how "socio-cognitive complexity" surfaces in a number of comics and graphic novels. Shklovsky's classic account of "art as technique" presents the notion that denaturalization is at the root of literariness, and his essay on *Tristram Shandy* applies this notion to Sterne's novel.

References

Austen, Jane. 2006 (1811). *Sense and Sensibility*. London: Penguin.

Brontë, Emily. 2010 (1847). *Wuthering Heights*. London: Harper.

Fuchs, Wolfgang and Reinold Reitberger. 1972. *Comics: Anatomy of a Mass Medium*. London: Studio Vista.

Jenkins, Henry, 2006. *Convergence Culture: Where Old and New Media Collide*. New York: New York University Press.

Jones, William B. Jr. 2011. *Classics Illustrated: A Cultural History*. 2nd edition. Jefferson, NC: McFarland.

Sabin, Roger. 2003. "Ally Sloper: The First Comics Superstar?" *Image and Narrative*, 7. Last accessed: October 15, 2012. http://www.imageandnarrative.be/inarchive/graphicnovel/rogersabin.htm (09 April 2013)

Shklovsky, Viktor. 1965. "Art as Technique" and "Sterne's *Tristram Shandy*: Stylistic Commentary." In *Russian Formalist Criticism: Four Essays*, 3–24 and 25–57. Lincoln: University of Nebraska Press.

Sterne, Laurence. 2009 (1759–67). *The Life and Opinions of Tristram Shandy, Gentleman*. Oxford: Oxford University Press.

Zunshine, Lisa. 2011. "What to Expect When You Pick Up A Graphic Novel" *SubStance*, 40.1: 114–34.

Comics Discussed

Austen, Jane. 2010. *Sense and Sensibility*. Adapted by Nancy Butler. Illustrated by Sonny Liew. New York: Marvel Comics.

Brontë, Emily. 2009. *Classics Illustrated 10: Wuthering Heights*. Adapted by Harry Miller. Illustrated by Henry C. Kiefer. Thatcham: Classic Comic Store.

Rowson, Martin. 2010. *The Life and Opinions of Tristram Shandy, Gentleman.* London: SelfMadeHero.
Sikoryak, Robert. 2009. *Masterpiece Comics.* Montreal: Drawn and Quarterly.

Class Activity 4: The Pitch

Get together in small groups, and agree on a novel you want to have adapted into a comic. Then prepare a pitch, as if for a comics publisher, outlining why this novel should be adapted, how the adaptation could be interesting, in terms of media affordances and convergence culture, and why people would want to read it. Each group then presents its pitch to the rest of the class.

Writing Assignment 4

Take a comic, either from this chapter or from your own collection, which you think should be awarded a literary prize (such as the Man Booker Prize – but you can aim at less prestigious competitions, too). Make a case for the committee why this comic deserves the recognition of a literary prize. Why should this comic be awarded a prize that is usually given to novels? Think of aesthetic, cultural, and commercial reasons, and consider media affordances. What aspect of the comic (stylistic sophistication, cultural relevance, etc.) do you want to stress? Write 300–500 words.

Essay Question 4

Poetic Metaphors in Rowson's *Tristram Shandy*

Apart from socio-cognitive complexity and defamiliarization, a third marker of literariness is quite pronounced in Martin Rowson's rendition of *Tristram Shandy*: poetic metaphor. Poetic metaphor refers to new and unexpected combinations between two conceptual domains. In comics, these can be realized in image combinations or in image-word combinations (see the brief discussion of metaphors in Chapter 1).

Consider how Rowson takes up verbal metaphors from *Tristram Shandy* in his graphic novel. When does he visualize verbal metaphors?

When does he add a second conceptual domain in the images to verbal discourse from *Tristram Shandy*, which was not obviously metaphorical on its own? What are the effects of the metaphors in Rowson's graphic novel? Can you discern a pattern or a dominant strategy of Rowson's? How do you think these metaphors affect the reader's evaluation of the graphic novel's literariness?

Additional reading

Lakoff, George and Mark Turner. 1989. *More Than Cool Reason: A Field Guide to Poetic Metaphor*. Chicago: University of Chicago Press.

5

Comics and Their History

Comics not only tell stories, express the personal experiences of their authors and interact with other media, as we discussed in the previous chapters. Comics also emerge from a particular historical situation. In this chapter, we will talk about the history of comics. The status of comics as popular culture has been the decisive social and cultural condition of English-language comics in the twentieth century, and this chapter will tell the history of comics through their relation to popular mass culture. Even though its roots go back into ancient art, the medium of comics (as I understand it here) only emerged at the turn of the twentieth century in newspapers and magazines. They were produced in cheap and disposable formats, and neither creating nor reading comics gathered much cultural prestige. In fact, comics were attacked as dangerously popular and had to submit to self-censorship. Toward the end of the twentieth century, comics began to outgrow these limitations of popular culture.

The Beginnings of Comics History

As writers on comics attempt to outline a history of comics, they often identify culturally significant texts as the precursors of comics. The murals of Ancient Egypt, Trajan's column, or the Bayeux tapestry have all been mentioned as instances of "early comics" with their sequences of visual narration and their combination of word and image. The idea that you can tell a story with images in sequence and that you can complement the visual information with written words has been around for a long time. However, is this enough to call the Bayeux tapestry a comic? Are image sequences and written words sufficient

Studying Comics and Graphic Novels, First Edition. Karin Kukkonen.
© 2013 John Wiley & Sons, Ltd. Published 2013 by John Wiley & Sons, Ltd.

evidence for describing this embroidered cloth from the Middle Ages as a comic? There are two things which distinguish the Bayeux tapestry from comics: first, comics segment their image sequences into panels and they integrate the written language in speech bubbles and captions. Second, comics are printed and reproduced on a large scale, but there is only one hand-embroidered Bayeux tapestry.

The medium-specific elements of comics, such as speech bubbles and panels, can be found much earlier than the twentieth century. In the Memorial Portrait of Sir Henry Unton of 1596 (Figure 5.1),[1] we see a sequence of images. This sequence is partitioned by rivers, rooms, and other elements of the setting. We could call these partitions "proto-panels," because the canvas is divided up into separate, sequential images. The story of Henry Unton's life begins in the bottom right-hand corner of the painting, we then follow the stream of figures into the house, and we see his exploits on the Grand Tour and in military service in the top images. His death is represented in the square image at the topic. His coffin is taken back, along the river, into the house, until the funeral procession moves it into the church to the left. The painting organizes its panels along rivers and moving figures (not dissimilar to Figure 1.6), which makes the sequence readable despite the unusual right-to-left direction. We can also find "proto-speech bubbles" early on in the traditions of visual narration. Medieval illuminated manuscripts often made use of scrolls emanating from the speaker's hands or head in order to integrate

Figure 5.1   NPG 710. Sir Henry Unton. *Source:* NPG 710. Sir Henry Unton by Unknown artist. Oil on panel, circa 1596. © National Portrait Gallery, London.

Figure 5.2 From *Horae Beatae Mariae Virginis. Source:* by Permission of University of Glasgow Library, Special Collections.

key phrases into their illustrations. A biblical illustration of the Annunciation, for example (Figure 5.2), shows Gabriel greeting Mary. The angel's "Ave Maria" is written onto a scroll which is connected to his hands. Both the scroll and contemporary speech bubbles work as visualizations of the conceptual metaphor that communication is a conduit through which messages are exchanged (see Chapter 1). Because this conceptual metaphor is a highly successful device for ordering experience and making sense of the world, and quite likely, has a very long history, it is not surprising that such "conduits" were used to integrate written text into visual narration across centuries. In the medieval illustrations, it occurs as a scroll; in contemporary comics, it occurs as a speech bubble.

Nevertheless, even though they use identifiable paneling and precursors to the speech bubble, neither Sir Henry Unton's portrait nor the medieval manuscript can really be called a comic. Comics are reproduced in large numbers through printing and then widely distributed. Sir Henry Unton's portrait and the medieval manuscript are hand-crafted and only a single copy of them exists. In terms of our definition of the medium, this means that even though both texts display the modalities of the comic, they do not feature its technology nor its institutions. The technology of the medium and its institutions work together as the production context of the medium, and this production context is different for comics and PROTO-COMICS. Even though the texts might look similar to comics, their modes of production are decisively different. Comics as a medium are tied to the modes of production of the popular mass culture of the twentieth century.

After our short excursion into the (potentially) long history of proto-comics, we can now refine our definition of comics: comics are a medium narrating through images, words, and panel sequences, and they emerge from the production context of popular mass culture of the twentieth century.

Precursors in Emergent Mass Culture

Since comics generally are produced en masse through cheap printing and circulated in newspapers, pamphlets, and trade paperbacks, they are clearly tied to popular mass culture. The rise of popular mass media seems to be the place to start a history of comics and precursors of today's comics can be found in political cartoons, satirical drawings, and the Sunday pages of newspapers.

Political cartoons, which were published in newspapers and satirical magazines in English-speaking countries, have featured speech bubbles and speed lines since the mid-nineteenth century. William Hogarth (1697–1764) drew satirical picture stories like *The Harlot's Progress* (1732) and *The Rake's Progress* (1735) in the tradition of earlier religious and moralistic pamphlets. Hogarth's picture stories were reproduced as engravings and widely circulated. They feature a number of striking scenes, which are explained and described in written text at the bottom (in the engravings). Later on, in the nineteenth century, the picture stories became more similar to comics as we know them. The German writer and illustrator Wilhelm Busch (1832–1908) combined various scenes and his satirical comments on a page, for example in *Max und Moritz* (1865). The Swiss writer and illustrator Rodolphe Töpffer (1799–1846) combined his images into sequences, employed speech bubbles, and the limited drawing style of caricature.

Rodolphe Töpffer was a comics writer who reflected on his medium, and his *Essai de physiognomie* (1845) offered many insights into characterization in comics (see Chapter 1). Some of Rodolphe Töpffer's stories were published in European newspapers and, by the 1840s, they were also introduced in US newspapers.

Humorous comics would be published in the magazines of the late nineteenth and early twentieth centuries (such as *Life* or *Harper's Monthly*), and later in the newspapers. The newspapers of the turn of the twentieth century had large Sunday extras for the amusement and edification of their readers. These Sunday pages featured entertaining stories with illustrating images and page layout (often) in four-color print. They also presented sumptuous illustrations of fashionable fantasies like Nell Brinkley's work (see Robbins, 2001) and information about life in the city in detailed drawings, such as "The Busiest Hour on Earth" (in *New York World* June 17, 1906); in which everything that happens in an hour in Manhattan is drawn on the face of a clock (see Baker and Brentano, 2005). A significant series of entertaining stories was Winsor McCay's weekly *A Tale of the Jungle Imps*, which ran in various US newspapers in 1903. His illustrations reflected the lavish newspaper layout of the Sunday pages and offered early examples of panel arrangement and layering. All these comics precursors to comics were published in pamphlets, newspapers, or illustrated books that were aimed at the emerging mass market.

Newspaper Comics (1900s–1930s)

At the beginning of the twentieth century, comics became a fixture in newspapers. The adventures of Richard F. Outcault's character The Yellow Kid (see Figure 5.4 on page 106) were published in various series in newspapers first of the Pulitzer and then of the Hearst syndicate in the United States, most prominently *Hogan's Alley* (1895–98). Like McCay's *Jungle Imps*, the comics featuring the Yellow Kid combined at first word blocks and drawn images, and only later developed the well-known panel-by-panel format with written text included through speech bubbles and captions. Rudolph Dirks's and Harold H. Knerr's series *The Katzenjammer Kids* (1897–1949) and George Herriman's Krazy Kat (1913–1944) further pioneered the comics form in newspapers. In the United Kingdom, Charles Ross's Ally Sloper made his debut in the humor magazine *Judy* in 1867. *Ally Sloper's Half Holiday*, which developed out of this series, was the first full comics magazine to be published

(1884–1916). It featured the adventures of Ally Sloper, as well as other comics and short narratives in black-and-white print. Like the Yellow Kid, Ally Sloper was a very popular character at its time, and both these comics formed important hinge points between the earlier cartoon with their individual images and separate texts, conventions familiar from editorial cartoons, and comics as we know them today.

At the beginning of the twentieth century, we have comics in place as a medium. On the Sunday pages of American newspapers, artists like Winsor McCay developed comics further. His series *Little Nemo in Slumberland* (1905–14) expands the possibilities of panel arrangement and page layout. The large format of the Sunday papers gives McCay's gorgeous and detailed drawings much room to explore what could be done with panel-sizes, cadres, and their arrangement on the page. *Little Nemo in Slumberland* is certainly one of the high points of the early newspaper comics and remains a touchstone of comics storytelling today (see Chapter 6). An alternative publication format for newspaper comics was the serialization in black-and-white daily strips and colored Sunday pages. Milton Caniff's *Terry and the Pirates* (1934–46), Alex Raymond's *Flash Gordon* (1934–43) and Hal Forster's *Prince Valiant* (1937–71) were published in this format and continued by other authors after their creators' tenure.

Early newspaper comics like *The Yellow Kid*, *The Katzenjammer Kids*, or *Little Nemo in Slumberland* reflect the emerging mass culture of the twentieth century. Never before had so many people lived in cities, and the sheer mass of people to be housed, occupied, and entertained changed the city landscape significantly. Architecture and city planning made their impact on the image and experience of the city. Advertisements in newspapers and on billboards addressed millions as potential customers and consumers. Zoos and amusement parks were new environments to be explored. All these changes connected to mass culture were referred to and discussed in the early newspaper comics: Winsor McCay's *Little Nemo in Slumberland* has to find his way in disorienting city landscapes (Figure 5.3), lives through adventures with exotic (zoo) animals and moves through fantastic architecture reminiscent of amusement parks and exhibitions. The dreamer in McCay's *Dreams of the Rarebit Fiend* is often caught up in the busy, fast-paced city life. In McCay's comics, billboards come to life and interact with the city dwellers. Richard F. Outcault's *Yellow Kid* takes the claims of hyperbolic advertisement to their absurd extreme (Figure 5.4). Comics are not only a medium of twentieth-century popular mass culture, but they also share the experience of living in these social and political contexts.

Figure 5.3 Little Nemo (I). (1907). *Source*: SFCGA - San Francisco Academy of Comic Art Collection, The Ohio State University Billy Ireland Cartoon Library and Museum.

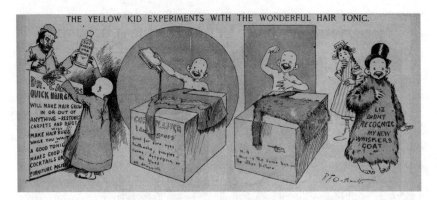

Figure 5.4   The Yellow Kid (1898). *Source*: SFCGA - San Francisco Academy of Comic Art Collection, The Ohio State University Billy Ireland Cartoon Library and Museum.

The Comic Book (1930–54)

In the United States, the comic book began its success story as a promotional give-away. Newspaper comics were reprinted in magazine-format publications, most famously *Funnies on Parade* (1933), and distributed to advertise other products. Soon, publishers realized that these comic books could be sold as a commodity in their own right. In the early comic book, genres and commercial practices from pulp magazines were adopted. Pulp magazines featured popular narratives, such as Robert E. Howard's *Conan the Barbarian* (1932–36), *Doc Savage* (1933–49) and *The Shadow* (1931–49), which was to influence comics storytelling. Some of the pulp heroes, like Conan or The Shadow, were also adopted into comics. The comic book in the 1930s was a magazine-like publication with several stories, or parts of stories, as well as advertisements and letters to the editors. Produced as a magazine, they would be brought to newsstands on a regular publication schedule. The comic book was not published to last: mostly, it was read and then thrown away or swapped for another comic book. In the 1930s, comic books came a long way from promotional give-away to a publication format of their own, yet they were still considered a consumer good more than anything else.

At this point, we have not only the modalities of today's comics, but also their material form of the magazine issue in place. Then something happened which would define the comics as a medium almost as much as their modalities and the magazine-form: the superheroes emerged. The first superhero was Superman in 1938, when the first story featuring this hero was published in a comic book called *Action Comics*. Superman soon got his own series and rival comics publishers brought their own superheroes to the market. After Superman, many other classic superheroes like Batman (1939), Wonder Woman (1941), and The Flash (1940) appeared within a couple of years. The period after 1938 is commonly called the Golden Age of superhero comics: the superheroes were very popular, their comic books sold very well, and comics artists produced new stories in a weekly rhythm. In the 1940s and 1950s, the superheroes became the dominant genre in comics with the greatest readership.

In the 1930s and 1940s, the comics medium in general was expanding enormously in terms of genres, target audiences and circulation. Comics had become a major cultural force in the United States. The average monthly circulation of comics rose from 17 million in 1940 to 70–100 million in 1953. By 1953, the American public spent over 1 billion dollars a year on comic books and about 90 percent of both boys and girls read them.[2] There were romance comics, which showed girls how to find Mr. Right, how to respond to male advances, and how to become a good wife. There were adventure and superhero comics for boys, which took them to exotic places and taught them about responsibility and the choices between good and evil. These comics were clearly informed by the morality of the 1950s and by the gender differences promoted between girls and boys in mass culture.

Another genre rose to importance in the late 1940s and early 1950s which followed quite different moral guidelines: the horror comic. Horror comics were highly popular and commercially successful, and many comics publishers produced horror series. The genre was pioneered by the comics publisher EC under its owner and editor William Gaines (1922–92). These horror comics featured stories of vampires, werewolves and ghouls, cannibalism, murder in the family, and being buried alive. They were usually introduced through distinct narrator figures like the Crypt-Keeper (in *Tales from the Crypt*), the Old Witch (in *The Haunt of Fear*) or the Vault Keeper (in *The Vault of Horror*), who maintain a strong presence throughout the story. Often, EC stories would experiment with a surprise twist to bring their story to an ending, just like our example in Chapter 2. *Watchmen* captures the horror comics' subject matter, visual style and narrative technique in *Tales of the Black Freighter*, a comic featured within its larger narrative (see Figure 5.5).

Figure 5.5 Tales of the Black Freighter. *Source:* from *Watchmen* © DC Comics. Used with Permission.

Box 5.1   *The Superheroes*

Superhero comics constitute what can be considered the comics genre par excellence. Their heroes save the world on a weekly basis, while they oscillate between (more or less) mundane alter egos, like Clark Kent, and hero personas of godlike perfection, like Superman. Each hero has a distinguishing costume and symbol (like the Batsign, for example), which marks out his or her particular identity. Across the twentieth century, superhero comics have moved from what comics fans have called the Golden Age (1938–late 1940s), in which many of the major heroes and the conventions of the genre were established, to the Silver Age (1956–1970s), in which more conflicted heroes like Spider-Man or the Hulk were introduced, on to an age of deconstruction (mid-1980s–1990s), in which their status as heroes and their right to install themselves as protectors of society was questioned, as in *Watchmen* (1986) or *Dark Knight Returns* (1986).

As the decades wore on after 1938, more and more different stories were told about the superhero characters and they were told by many different authors. This led to two consequences: first, the political interests and investments of the individual hero changes over time, while his role as a hero remains the same. In this sense, the superheroes serve as a modern mythology, as Richard Reynolds (1992) and Umberto Eco (1972) suggest in now classical assessments of the superhero genre. Second, the storylines of the heroes got more and more confusing, and continuity became an issue. As new authors take over an established superhero series, they often "retcon" this hero, that is they retell his origin story to suit (their) new narratives which might not fit the old version. Different versions of the same character emerge, like the old and new Night Owl in *Watchmen*. Comics like *Crisis on Infinite Earths* (1985) propose that the different versions of the superheroes are located in different fictional worlds, alternative realities within the so-called "MULTIVERSE." Crisis resets the history of the DC Universe by having these worlds collapse. Since then, however, the worlds have proliferated and the multiverse has emerged again. In *Watchmen*, different superhero generations are brought together, as the optimistic heroes of the Golden Age encounter the more cynical and conflicted heroes of the Silver Age, and different versions of the same character, like the two Night Owls, meet. *Watchmen* addresses changing political involvements, asksthe question of what it means to be a (super-)hero, and thereby reflects on the superhero comics as a complex and challenging genre.

Comics Censorship (1954)

Comics' wide popularity, their huge commercial success and the carefree exploitation in many of their stories started a large debate about comics and their educational and cultural value in the United States as the 1950s began. Parents, politicians, and psychologists became concerned about the comics American children were reading. Was reading comics harmless entertainment? Or did the depiction of sordid crimes and scary events, especially in the horror comics, lead to the moral deterioration of children's minds and eventually to juvenile delinquency?

These concerns of parents and politicians were championed by child psychologist Fredric Wertham (1895–1981). Wertham had analyzed comics for their impact on children's thinking and he conducted a number of interviews among his young patients to confirm his assumptions. He also was a man able to write colorful prose and was not afraid to speak his mind. In his book *The Seduction of the Innocent* (1954), Wertham brings both together: *The Seduction of the Innocent* diagnoses a disease, namely juvenile delinquency and (seemingly) rampant moral deterioration of the younger generation, and traces it back to a virus, namely comics and their unsavory stories. Wertham carries the disease-metaphor further, when he describes how the virus of comics has been spreading in a friendly environment and when he emphasizes that it is now time a doctor stepped in and provided a remedy. That doctor was to be Dr. Fredric Wertham.

Comics fans often perceive of Wertham as a conservative fear-monger, but it was not Wertham's *Seduction of the Innocent* alone that brought about comics censorship. Larger social currents like the parents' aim to control emergent youth culture and the rise of cultural criticism in the United States carried the move against comics (see Beaty 2005). Wertham wrote a fiery book against comics with *The Seduction of the Innocent*, which then became a symbol of this campaign. By 1954, the public discussion about comics and their influence on adolescent minds and morals had gained enough momentum for senate hearings to be opened, which were to investigate the effects of comic books on juvenile delinquency. The commission invited Fredric Wertham, as an expert on the psychological effects of comics, as well as several representatives of the comics industry to make their case. Among the representatives of the comics industry was William Gaines, the editor and owner of the horror comics publishing house EC. William Gaines took much of the spotlight in these hearings, not only because he represented horror comics, the most disreputable genre, but also because he fought back against Fredric Wertham and those concerned about the impact of comics (see Box 5.2).

A strong enough link between comics and juvenile delinquency was not proven for the government to establish official censorship on comics. The comics industry, however, considered itself to have entered troubled waters, and in order to regain the trust of the public and to save their industry, the CMAA, the Comics Magazine Association of America, decided to install self-censorship in September 1954. A set of standards were established to which any comic book had to comply. By the end of October 1954, these standards were published as The Comics Code, and from then on, new comic books would be sent to the office of the Comics Code Authority for inspection. If the Comics Code Authority decided that the comic satisfied the demands of the Comics Code, they put the seal of approval on the comic's cover.

The Comics Code specified that comics should be without sexually suggestive imagery, blood, gore and violence, and without any escape from justice for criminals. The classic EC plot, in which an attractive woman would be gagged and bound, in which body parts were used for impromptu baseball games, in which the child murdering its parents is never caught, were no longer possible. The Comics Code certainly affected comics genres other than the horror comics. It restrained the storytelling options of superhero comics and adventure comics, and led to a reorientation in the advertisement sections of the comic books. However, for no other genre was the Comics Code as decisive: since horror comics thrived on everything which the Code forbade – sexual tension, gory deeds, and illicit outcomes – none of the EC comics could hope to pass the inspection of the Comics Code Authority. William Gaines and EC comics did not join the Comics Code Authority and their comics were not submitted for inspection. However, after only a few months, EC had to stop publishing its horror titles, because distributors and news vendors would no longer accept EC comic books for sale. Without the stamp of the CCA, no news vendor wanted these comic books on his or her stand. And without anyone to sell their comics, EC was almost shut down. Only one of their comic books continues to be published today, the satirical magazine *MAD*.

Box 5.2 *What happened at the Senate Hearings*

At the Senate hearings, Fredric Wertham mounted a well-laid out and poignant attack on comics when he addressed the commission. "Hitler was a beginner compared to the comic book industry," he said, implying that the indoctrination of young Americans through comic books was comparable to the propaganda on which Hitler built his totalitarian state in Germany. According to Wertham, comics are not seemingly harmless entertainment, but work on the minds of their readers, much like propaganda. William Gaines, who had seen literally hundreds of horror stories through production as EC's editor, retorted, saying "it would be just as difficult to explain the harmless thrill of a horror story to a Dr. Wertham as it would be to explain the sublimity of love to a frigid old maid." In other words, Dr. Wertham does obviously not enjoy reading horror comics, so how could he ever understand what attracts their readers? All the parents, politicians, and psychologists who are concerned about horror comics being nothing but blood and gore simply do not get them, was Gaines's argument. That might have been the case, but Gaines was playing a losing game when he implicitly claimed that the majority of the people in the Senate commission had no idea what they were judging. Once the senators brought out some of the EC comic books he had edited and asked him to explain "the harmless thrill of a horror story," he was in trouble.

The debate between Gaines and the senators revolved around the criterion of "taste." The senators tried to establish EC Comics as products of popular culture, exploiting readers' fascination with the macabre, and making good money from it. In one of the most frequently quoted passages from the hearings, Gaines and the senators quibble over whether this cover (Figure 5.6) is "in good taste." "Taste" is the reaction of our palate to food – being delighted or repulsed. In the debate, taste is used metaphorically to refer to the capacity to make aesthetic judgments and to discern the culturally acceptable. Because of its metaphorical relation to an immediate physical sensation, "taste" seems obvious and easy to agree upon, when in fact, in cultural terms, it relies to a large degree on the ground rules for desirable achievements established by society itself.

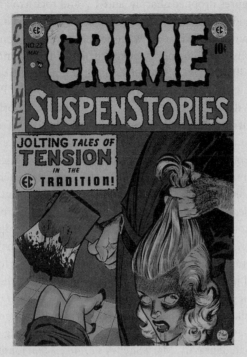

Figure 5.6 Crime Suspenstories (1954). EC logo™ and image © Wm. M. Gaines, Agent, Inc. 2012. All rights reserved.

The ground rules of art for the senator are inoffensive subject matter and no commercial interest. Both these features, however, have developed historically, as cultural value hierarchies were negotiated and their importance is by no means as natural as the reaction of our taste buds. (You can read the transcript of Gaines' testimony at the Senate Hearings here: http://www.thecomicbooks.com/gaines.html.)

Comics as Popular Culture

In the 1930s, comics had become the key entertainment medium in the United States, but the concern of parents, politicians, and psychologists brought their popularity to an end. After 1954 and the introduction of the Comics Code, the comics sales figures dropped sharply, and TV and rock'n'roll took over as the most worrying juvenile vice. Being a popular medium seems to have brought about the undoing of comics. But what does it mean that comics are popular culture? And why should being "popular" turn into a problem?

Raymond Williams, one of the most important people to write on popular culture, has an entry on "popular" in his *Keywords* (1976). "Popular culture," according to Williams comes to mean "inferior kinds of work" produced "to win favour," but also "well-liked" cultural products (199). For comics in the first half of the twentieth century, both these meanings are accurate. Since about 90 percent of boys and girls in the United read comic books in 1953, we can certainly assume that they were "well-liked." However, they were also considered "inferior kinds of work," as the concern of parents, the argument in Wertham's *Seduction of the Innocent* and the Senate hearings proved. This assumed inferiority in quality justified their strict censorship by the Comics Code Authority. Wertham also mentions comics adaptations of literary classics disapprovingly, but their publishers Dell and Gilberton (for *Classics Illustrated*) did not suffer as much from opting out from the Comics Code, even though they published stories like Robert Stevenson's *Dr. Jekyll and Mr. Hyde*, Bram Stoker's *Dracula* and Mary Shelley's *Frankenstein*. These literary classics broke several rules of the Comics Code by including monsters, vampires, and human depravity. Mary Shelley's *Frankenstein* for example features a morbidly obsessed scientist and a horrible monster assembled from the body parts of corpses, neither of which would be out of place in an EC comic. Still, we do not consider this novel popular trash, and a comic version of *Frankenstein* would not have to be approved by the CCA because it claims similar cultural prestige as Shelley's novel. The difference between the Mary Shelley's *Frankenstein* and the average EC comic has to do with the value hierarchy between high culture and popular culture. We ascribe certain values to different texts.

There are several ways in which it can be argued that *Frankenstein* is a piece of literary art. First, the novel presents to its readers a complex and multifaceted account of the ambition and anguish of the scientist Dr. Viktor Frankenstein and the despair and craftiness of his creature. Second, Mary Shelley ties her story in with the larger cultural heritage of the Western world. The full title of her novel is *Frankenstein, or A Modern Prometheus*. Prometheus is one of the titans of Greek mythology. He was the one who stole fire from the gods, brought it to humanity, and thus started the development of human culture. With her subtitle, Shelley puts Viktor Frankenstein in the tradition of culture heroes who aimed to improve the development and progress of humanity, such as Prometheus or Dr. Faustus. Third, Mary Shelley was the wife of Percy Bysshe Shelley, who was one of the most important English Romantics, as well as the daughter of Mary Wollstonecraft, one of the first feminist authors, and William Godwin, a well-noted radical writer at the turn of the nineteenth century. So, the quality of the work itself, the fact that it is inscribed into the tradition of the culture hero (as well as other larger cultural narratives) and Shelley's biographical connection to literary history, led to the novel *Frankenstein* being considered a piece of high culture. As *Frankenstein* is featured in the classics editions of book publishers, and as the novel is discussed in English literature classes, this high culture status is reinforced by the novel's reception.

The value of high culture is actually only to some extent tied to the quality of the text, to how well it engages and entertains its readers. A good part of the difference between "high culture" and "popular culture" has to do with the contexts of publication and reception, within which the value judgment is ascribed. The medium and the context of a text do not determine the quality of the text, but they do determine our expectations towards the text. You expect important pieces of art in a gallery – and not meaningless rubbish – because it is a place of high culture. You expect repetitive and exploitative stories in comics, because comics are a medium of popular culture. The comics distributors would have had no qualms distributing a Classics Illustrated version of *Frankenstein*, because the novel was considered high culture and the series stressed its fidelity to the literary classic.

For an enquiry of how such expectations come about and what these value judgments are based on, we have to go back again to the nineteenth century and to the beginning of popular mass culture. There was popular culture well before the nineteenth century – it was the culture of the people as opposed to the culture of the court or the culture of nobility. It was largely oral and not put into handwritten codices or painted on cathedral walls. From the eighteenth century onwards, with the industrialization and general education, newspapers and pamphlets could be mass-produced through the printing press and distributed to a larger audience; potentially to anyone who could read the language. You have seen how the experience of twentieth-century mass culture was reflected in the early newspaper comics, such as *The Yellow Kid* or *Little Nemo in Slumberland*. When mass-culture emerged in the second half of the nineteenth century, key ideas of what is culture and what functions it serves were also developed.

The British cultural critic Matthew Arnold (1822–88) was concerned that if people read nothing but newspapers, they would lose the ability to reflect on their thinking and the incremental growth of personality which the sustained engagement with literary texts brings. He writes in the preface to his essay collection *Culture and Anarchy*:

> The whole scope of the essay is to recommend culture as the great help of our present difficulties; culture being a pursuit of our total perfection by means of getting to know, on all the matters which much concern us, the best which has been thought and said in the world, and, through this knowledge, turning a stream of fresh and free thought upon our stock notions and habits, which we now follow staunchly but mechanically, vainly imagining that there is a virtue in following them staunchly which makes up for the mischief of following them mechanically. (2009, 5)

Arnold sees culture as an active force for a better society. It is not only "the best which has been thought and said in the world," but should bring out the best in us and lead society in its "pursuit of total perfection." While Arnold himself, with his emphasis on a common culture for all social classes, might not have been elitist, the definition of culture he popularized in *Culture and Anarchy* could easily be turned into an elitist argument against comics, as soon as one assumed that comics would detract from the lofty function of literature that Arnold outlines.

Comics as the product of popular mass culture, printed on cheap paper, sold and distributed weekly, and designed to be thrown away after reading, indeed seem a far cry from "the best which has been thought and said in the world." As common prejudice has it, popular culture is formulaic, simplistic, and banal; it does not make you think about the important things in life and educate your mind toward "perfection." On the contrary, it potentially deteriorates your mind and prevents you from being a critical citizen, as it whisks you away into fantasy worlds. This was the conclusion which the critics of the FRANKFURT SCHOOL drew. The Frankfurt School is a group of cultural critics like Max Horkheimer, Theodor Adorno, and Jürgen Habermas. They were suspicious of mass culture, because they saw first-hand what the mass culture of the Nazi regime did to Germany and to Germany's public culture in the 1930s. The Frankfurt School assumed that the (mass) culture industry works largely to soothe its consumers, to provide cheap and gratifying entertainment, and to keep them from participating in the political discussion of the day. High culture (which can be subject to a culture industry as well) is generally supposed to stimulate the critical mind of the citizen and serve as the example of "the best that has been thought and said in the world." Popular culture, on the other hand, distracts from these goals and can become at worst a threat to democratic societies, and at best an endless circle of supply and demand in escapist entertainment.

Both the arguments of Arnold and the arguments of the Frankfurt School proved very successful. They inform how we consider popular culture: it is trivial, gratifying, and does not engage critically. These were the features through which the texts of mass media like TV, films, and comics, came to be seen, and they have stuck ever since.

Breaking the Code 1: Pop Art and Underground Comix

After 1954, the comics industry largely abided by the Comics Code and aimed to produce inoffensive stories. Comics would never again achieve the cultural currency they had in the 1930s and 1940s. Circulation figures plummeted in the 1950s. While the comics industry was struggling, comics themselves made their way into other fields in the 1960s. The art scene took up comics, their speech bubbles, speed-lines, and grainy print, as an aesthetic expression. Pop artists like Roy Lichtenstein recreated comics panels on canvas and presented them in exhibition. For the first time, perhaps, comics were featured in venues of high culture like museums and art galleries. The pop-artists were out to shock the art establishment and to unmask the value hierarchy between high culture and popular culture. They first and foremost conceived of comics as an instance of consumer culture; a disposable, everyday commodity. Comics were considered on a par with the soup tins and cleaning devices which Andy Warhol famously painted in his Campbell's soup tins and recreated as a statue with his Brillo boxes. Pop art was not so much interested in developing comics as a medium as they were in using them to rattle the cages of the art establishment.

Underground comix emerged in the 1960s with a similarly subversive intention. The authors of underground comix understood comics as a medium in which they could express themselves and their concerns. Underground comix would also flagrantly break the Comics Code; Robert Crumb, for example, freely features sexual intercourse and drug use in his series *Fritz the Cat* (1965–72). Neither the personalized drawing styles nor the breaking of the Comics Code were something that could be realized within the confines of the comics industry. Underground comix thus relied on self-publication and self-distribution. Because people like Robert Crumb would print and distribute their comics themselves, they did not have to submit their comics for inspection to the Comics Code Authority. Underground comix developed highly personalized drawing styles and idiosyncratic narrative voices, and thus became forerunners of the autobiographical comics (see Chapter 3).

Breaking the Code 2: The British Invasion

On the level of mainstream comics, the Comics Code remains in effect until today – in principle. Yet, by and by, also mainstream comics have emancipated themselves from the Comics Code Authority, and a large proportion of their comics is not submitted for inspection anymore. In 1971, Marvel broke the Comics Code with issue #96 of *The Amazing Spider-Man*. Marvel was commissioned by the US Department of Health to produce a story showing the problems of drug abuse. For this, the comic of course had to represent drug abuse, which was something that the Comics Code did not allow. However, the fact that a US Department commissioned the story goes to show that by the 1970s the Comics Code was not taken seriously anymore. Marvel was the first major comics publishing house to break the self-censorship of the Comics Code, but differently from the underground comics, it did so well within the approval of mainstream society.

Soon enough, other comics publishers would also decide to publish series for more grown-up readers, which they did not submit to the Comics Code Authority. A crucial factor in this development was the so-called "BRITISH INVASION." The British Invasion in comics refers to the significant influence of British authors and illustrators on the development of US comics from the 1980s. In music, the term British Invasion refers to the way in which British musicians like the Beatles, the Rolling Stones, and David Bowie dominated the US music scene in the 1960s and 1970s. A second British Invasion in the 1980s would reshape English-language mainstream comics.

In the 1980s, both DC and Marvel decided to relaunch their major series, and they contracted a large number of authors from the UK to write these new versions. Alan Moore took over the horror series *The Swamp Thing* in 1983. *The Swamp Thing* was the first mainstream comics series to be published without the Comics Code Authority's seal of approval. With the success of both these series, more Britons were hired by DC and Marvel, such as Neil Gaiman, Warren Ellis, and Grant Morrison. Their comics writing changed what comics were and explored what they could be. Alan Moore undertook a critical investigation of the superhero genre with his *Watchmen* of 1986. Neil Gaiman wrote a comics series that wins literary prizes with *The Sandman* (1989–95). Grant Morrison created a superhero comic that self-reflexively questions the role of author, reader, and hero, and pushed the comics form to its limits with *Animal*

Man (1988–90), and Warren Ellis produced a critical study of postmodern society with *Transmetropolitan* (1997–2000).

Under the influence of the British Invasion, English-language mainstream comics had become a medium for social commentary, which is self-reflexive of its own involvements with ideology and full of artistic complexity. There are certainly American comics authors who were important for comics in the 1980s, like Frank Miller who reimagined Batman in his *Dark Knight Returns* (1986). Yet the most influential writers of English-language comics at the end of the twentieth century are the comics authors of the British Invasion. To some extent, they undid the comics' confinement in popular culture. *Watchmen*, a key comic of the British Invasion, reflects on the tensions between high culture and popular culture. In particular the comic-within-the-comic, "Tales of the Black Freighter" (Figure 5.5), brings back both the narrative style and the social commentary of EC comics, and thereby shows a path which comics could have taken if it hadn't been for the self-censorship of the Comics Code.

* * *

When writing an account of comics history, you can posit different themes, and these themes will determine where and when your history starts, which developments you consider important and which conclusions you come to. For this chapter, I have focused on comics as a medium of popular culture. I therefore stressed the importance of technologies and institutions over the modalities of the medium, and my comics history does not start long before the twentieth century. Other approaches to comics history might make different decisions and have different ideas about what is important in comics history (see the introduction to Walker 2004 for an outline of other approaches).

As a part of popular mass culture, comics emerged at the turn of the twentieth century. They reflected the new urban experience of the early twentieth century. They were cheap, disposable entertainment that proliferated from the humorous newspaper comics to the adventure, romance, horror, and superhero comic books. Their popular culture status and exploitative appeal led to parental concerns and self-censorship in the middle of the century, and to a low status in the hierarchy of cultural value judgments. The second half of the twentieth century saw comics renegotiating their popular culture status through underground and alternative comics, as well as the ambitious and self-reflexive narratives of the authors of the British Invasion.

Notes

1   I am grateful to Ben Little for pointing me toward Sir Henry Unton.
2   The statistics are taken from Wright 2001.

Recommended Reading

Kunzle, David. 1973 and 1990. *The Early Comic Strip*. Berkeley: University of California Press.

Vol.1 Narrative Strips and Picture Stories in the European Broadsheet
Vol.2 The Nineteenth Century.

Sabin, Roger. 1996. *Comics, Comix and Graphic Novels*. London: Phaidon.
Walker, Brian. 2004. *The Comics Before 1945*. New York: N.H. Abrams.
Baker, Nicholson and Margaret Brentano. 2005. *The World on Sunday: Graphic Art in Joseph Pullitzer's Newspaper (1898–1911)*. New York: Bulfinch Press.

Kunzle's book provides a detailed overview on how the comics means of expression like visual sequence, speech bubbles, etc., have developed in earlier media. Sabin provides a broad account of comics in the twentieth century, especially underground and alternative comics. Walker's volumes are colorful overviews, featuring newspaper comics in particular.

Wright, Bradford W. 2001. *Comic Book Nation: The Transformation of Youth Culture in America*. Baltimore: Johns Hopkins University Press.
Gordon, Ian. 1998. *Comic Strips and Consumer Culture, 1890–1945*. Washington, DC: Smithsonian Institution Press.
Lopes, Paul. 2009. *Demanding Respect: The Evolution of the American Comic Book*. Philadelphia: Temple University Press.
Nyberg, Amy Kiste. 1998. *Seal of Approval: The History of the Comics Code*. Jackson: University of Mississippi Press.
Beaty, Bart. 2005. *Fredric Wertham and the Critique of Mass Culture*. Jackson: University of Mississippi Press.

Wright and Gordon provide each a detailed historical account of the comic book in US popular culture in the twentieth century. Lopes retells the history of the comic book as a process of cultural valorization. Nyberg and Beaty focus on the critique of comic books in the 1950s and the cultural impact of the Comics Code.

Chabon, Michael. 2000. *The Amazing Adventures of Kavalier and Clay*. New York: Random House.

Chabon's novel tells a gripping fictional version of the comics' success in the first half of the twentieth century, modeled on the life stories of the Superman creators Joe Shuster and Jerry Siegel, as well as Will Eisner.

If you want to learn more about popular culture, look at:

Williams, Raymond. 1976. *Keywords: A Vocabulary of Culture and Society*. London: Croom Helm.
Frow, Jonathan. 1995. *Cultural Studies and Cultural Value*. Oxford: Oxford University Press.
Arnold, Matthew. 2009. *Culture and Anarchy*. Edited by Jane Garnett. Oxford: Oxford University Press.
Adorno, Theodor. 2001. "Culture Industry Reconsidered." In *The Culture Industry: Selected Essays on Mass Culture*, 98–101. London: Routledge.

Raymond Williams' entries on "popular" and "culture" in his *Keywords* provides a good first glance at the value judgments surrounding popular culture. Jonathan Frow's discussion of popular culture is much more detailed. Frow also explains how today the value judgment between popular culture and high culture has diversified into multiple cultural fields. Arnold and Adorno provide you with the key statements of classical cultural criticism.

References

Arnold, Matthew. 2009. *Culture and Anarchy*. Edited by Jane Garnett. Oxford: Oxford University Press.
Baker, Nicholson and Margaret Brentano. 2005. *The World on Sunday: Graphic Art in Joseph Pullitzer's Newspaper (1898–1911)*. New York: Bulfinch Press.
Beaty, Bart. 2005. *Fredric Wertham and the Critique of Mass Culture*. Jackson: University of Mississippi Press.
Eco, Umberto. 1972. "The Myth of Superman." *Diacritics*, 2.1: 14–22.
Reynolds, Richard. 1992. *Super Heroes: A Modern Mythology*. London: Batsford.
Robbins, Trina. 2001. *Nell Brinkley and the New Woman in the Early 20th Century*. Jefferson: McFarland.
Walker, Brian. 2004. *The Comics Before 1945*. New York: N.H. Abrams.
Williams, Raymond. 1976. *Keywords: A Vocabulary of Culture and Society*. London: Croom Helm.

Comics Discussed

Alan Moore. 1987. *Watchmen*. Illustrated by Dave Gibbons. New York: DC Comics.

Class Activity 5: Writing Comics History

Get together in groups. Start writing your own history of comics, an account alternative to what you have just read here. Which comics need to be part of that history? When would it start? When would it end? Which issues and topics would be the most important, the ones that guide your historical narrative?

Writing Assignment 5

Figure 5.5 is a page from "Tales of the Black Freighter" in *Watchmen*, in which a marooned sailor tries to find his way home in horrible conditions. Here, he has just arrived on the shores of his hometown. He suspects that the enemy has taken the town and killed his family. Imagine you are working for the Comics Code Authority and that you need to check whether this page conforms to the Comics Code. Look up the rules of the Comics Code. Would you give it the seal of approval of the Comics Code? Explain your decision and write 300–500 words.

Essay Question 5

Popular Culture in Watchmen
Watchmen is set in an alternative version of the United States in 1985. Within this storyworld, the characters encounter and comment upon several different media of popular culture. How do characters in *Watchmen* comment upon popular culture? How do they evaluate it? What are its functions in the society depicted in *Watchmen*?

What would Matthew Arnold or the members of the Frankfurt School have to say about *Watchmen's* presentation of popular culture? Where would they agree? Where would they disagree?

6

The Study and Criticism of Comics

In the previous chapters, I have outlined different aspects of the comics themselves: their elements, their storytelling, their relation to other media and their history. In this chapter, we will look more closely at different ways of talking about and of studying comics; the different kinds of resources you can tap into and the different kinds of critical approaches that have been brought to bear on comics. As you work toward your final essay, these resources and approaches can help you find a topic and explore it from different angles. The end of the section will provide an introduction on how to write an essay on comics and how to cite the comics sources you use for it.

Resources for Studying Comics

For studying comics, scholars have a wide range of resources available, and as comics begin to be taught in schools and continue to be introduced into university curricula, the amount and range of these resources is sure to grow. In this section, I will give you a brief guided tour through some of the resources available for studying and analyzing comics.

Access to Comics Texts

Each of the comics I discuss in this volume has an ISBN number and is distributed through international booksellers. In terms of access, comics like *Maus* or *Watchmen* are easy to acquire. Special editions such as *Metamaus*, a collection of background materials, taped testimony, and Spiegelman's reflections on

Studying Comics and Graphic Novels, First Edition. Karin Kukkonen.
© 2013 John Wiley & Sons, Ltd. Published 2013 by John Wiley & Sons, Ltd.

making *Maus*, or *Absolute Watchmen*, an oversized edition of Moore's comic with additional material provided by Gibbons and the original coloring from Higgins, are on the rise for the comics and graphic novels which have garnered most critical attention in recent years. These open up contemporary contexts, provide additional material on the creation process of the comics, and many other valuable sources of information.

But also older comics, which have been out of print for some time, are being reedited and made accessible to a readership beyond comic book collectors. Some examples are the new editions of George Herriman's *Krazy Kat* comics, either in the original broadsheet size (*A Celebration of Sundays*) or in complete works (by Fantagraphics), or the DC Archive Editions and Marvel Essentials, which republish superhero comics from the 1940s onwards, be they key figures in the genre (like Superman) or marginal characters (like the Black Canary, for example). Today, a broad array of newspaper comics and comic books, which had originally been published as a consumable good, to be read and thrown away, is available in new editions as well.

Another source for comics from the earlier periods of the medium's history are the libraries and archives which have specialized in comics. The Billy Ireland Cartoon Library and Museum at Ohio State University in Columbus, for example, stocks comics, the original cartoon drawings of the artists and secondary reading, and sets up related exhibitions. Much of their material, from sketches for political cartoons to Winsor McCay's work, is available for viewing in their online art database. This database is a good place to start if you want to immerse yourself in the history of comics. Among the many other libraries which archive comics material (and display some of it online) are the British Library (especially for early British comics like Ally Sloper), or the Library of the French Centre for Comics in Angoulême. Most European nations will have their own special library or collection devoted to comics. When looking for comics to browse or explore, don't forget your town library. Most local libraries stock a selection of comics and graphic novels for recreational reading.

Critical Work on Comics

The national comics centers and the comics research libraries also hold a wide selection of secondary reading, namely comics criticism and academic work on comics. Secondary reading on comics can be published in a variety of formats: as a book, as a journal article, or as a critical essay in a blog.

Academic books on comics are published across the spectrum of university presses and academic publishing houses. Usually, this is comics criticism employing the approach or falling within the discipline the publishing house specializes in. Academic publishers with a special interest in comics, and a large number of publications on comics, include the University Press of Mississippi and McFarland. Other academic publishing houses are beginning to launch book series like "Studies in Comics and Cartoons" at Ohio University Press.

By now there are also quite a few journals specializing in comics studies. Some of them take a stance informed by history and cultural studies, surveying the world-wide comics production, like *The International Journal of Comics Art*, or highlighting the production contexts of comics, like *Journal of Graphic Novels and Comics*. Other journals are more closely related to literary studies, like *The European Journal of Comic Art, Studies in Comics*, or *ImageText*. Some of these journals are only available by subscription or through your university library. Other journals like *ImageText* or *Image and Narrative* (which does not focus exclusively on comics) are open-access journals, whose articles are freely available online. Each of the journals has a web page which lists their back issues and the authors and titles of articles that have been published so far. They are a good indicator of what issues, approaches, and comics texts form the core of the current academic debate.

Various comics blogs or comics commentary sites are available on the web in huge numbers as well, posting critical essays on comics, comics production, or related issues, such as *The Comics Journal* (www.tcj.com). Some of this criticism is more interesting (and more accomplished) than the rest , but it is often worth having a look at to find out which new comics are being published and what people think about them. Also established national newspapers, like *The Guardian* or *The New York Times* now feature reviews of comics and graphic novels and post them on their web sites.

Web sites like ComicsResearch.org and neuviemeart.citebd.org list bibliographies of books on comics, journals on comics, conferences devoted to discussing research on comics, as well as links to many other web-based resources like libraries, encyclopedias, national comics organizations, or online discussion lists. As with the web pages on comics criticism, there is so much material available that it is sometimes confusing to find your way around. Larger, more established web pages, and pages which are regularly updated are probably the most reliable place to start.

Critical Approaches to Comics

Comics have only recently emerged as a field of academic study and there is not yet a critical approach that takes comics exclusively as it object. Instead, comics studies draw on a variety of other approaches that have been developed in literary study, linguistics, the social sciences, and psychology. As comics scholars address comics through these approaches, they adopt them for their object of research, and this contributes to a plurality of methods in comics studies. In this section, I will introduce six different approaches to comics through a reading of Winsor McCay's *Little Nemo in Slumberland*. Three of these approaches (semiotics, narratology, and cognitive study) focus on the text and lead to close readings; three approaches (historical and auteurist approaches, cultural studies and gender studies, and psychoanalysis) look at various contexts and tie comics into larger social and psychological narratives.

Comics Semiotics

Semiotics, the study of signs, aims to outline how signs contribute to our meaning-making process. The approach has been developed mainly for language, but from its very beginning, semiotics suggested that signs operate in all areas of cultural production, and that therefore not only literature, but also films, comics or even fashion could be the domain of semiotics. According to Saussurean semiotics, the sign relates a signifier (the word "cat") to a signified (our concept of "cat"). This relation is largely arbitrary and only becomes meaningful in relation to a language system. "Cat" is "chat" in French, "Katze" in German, and "kissa" in Finnish, and the individual words make only sense in relation to the larger system of these languages.

Comics semiotics therefore works towards outlining the system of signs in comics. In *The System of Comics* (2007), Thierry Groensteen suggests that the panel is the smallest (useful) unit of meaning-making on the page, and that panels and their elements (speech bubbles, gutters, etc.) relate to each other in meaningful and systematic ways on the page. Each of the elements has a particular set of functions it can be put to. Groensteen establishes an "arthrology," literally a "study of joints," for comics, which describes the way panels work together on the spatio-temporal field of the page. What he calls "restrained arthrology" refers to the panel-by-panel sequence of meaning-making; what he calls "braids" refers to repetitions and panel relations which do not rely strictly on sequence but create connections and thereby meaning across the page or even the entire comic.

This installment of Winsor McCay's *Little Nemo in Slumberland* series tells the story of how Little Nemo and his friends are getting lost in the "hall of befuddlement" on the quest for Nemo's friend, the Princess. A semiotics approach, in the parameters outlined by Groensteen, would look at the relative sizes of the panels and their arrangement on the page. The first panel shows the

Figure 6.1 Little Nemo (II). (1908). *Source:* WGCGA - Woody Gelman Collection, The Ohio State University Billy Ireland Cartoon Library and Museum.

boys in their regular size, but as the mirrors distort the proportions of their bodies in the following panels, also the panels themselves get progressively longer and bigger. The last one in this row almost covers the entire length of the page. In the second row, the panels start getting smaller again until the last panel is of the same size as the first panel. In the end, everything is back to normal. The relative size and shape of the panels, and their arrangement on the page, outlines the basic structure of meaning to readers.

Comics semiotics is worthwhile reading up on if you are interested in:

- the possible functions of the elements of the comics page
- their relation to each other in the layout of the comics page

Comics Narratology

Narratology, the study of narratives, has a similar interest in the building principles of comics as semiotics, but its emphasis lies in the stories that comics tell, rather than the localized meaning-making processes as such. Like semiotics, narratology understands the entirety of cultural production to be its domain and endeavors to provide a framework for analyzing narrative and storytelling in literature, films, comics, but also everyday encounters. Indeed, comics have sometimes served as an illustration and test case for narratological discussions. Seymour Chatman introduces the basic narratological distinction between story and discourse by discussing a comic strip in his book *Story and Discourse* (1980). The narrator in visual narratives, as opposed to verbal narratives, is a problem discussed in both films studies and comics studies. Edward Branigan's *Narrative Comprehension and Film* (1992) engages with focalization, the person-bound limitation of knowledge and experience in storytelling, for visual media through a comic. In more general terms, current narratology has developed a transmedial approach, which outlines the differences between media in features and affordances but works towards a common vocabulary and explanatory framework for all narratives.

The installment from *Little Nemo in Slumberland* presents each of the narrative segments we discussed in Chapter 2. The headline gives us a preview of what this is all about (abstract); the discussion of the boys in the first panel outlines the situation to us and what the boys are doing in this hall of mirrors in the first place (orientation); in the next panel, the boys run into trouble, when their bodies are distorted by the mirrors (conflicting action); they assess the situation (evaluation); yet it does not get resolved until the very last panel, when Little Nemo wakes up (resolution); and then the dialogue with his mother offers a conclusion to the narrative (coda). McCay builds here an arc of narrative tension that spans the installment and is complete within itself, yet it is still inscribed in a larger narrative, that of Little Nemo's explorations of Slumberland

and his quest for the Princess, which will be continued in the next Sunday's installment.

In this particular installment, McCay develops an interesting trick for rendering narrative perspective: the panel surfaces serve as semi-transparent mirrors, reflecting the storyworld back to itself but allowing readers to see into it at the same time. In the first panel, the mirror of the panel surface combines with another mirror behind the boys and creates endless lines of reflections. In the second panel, the boys seem to look at the reader, and they see (in the mirror) what the reader is seeing (in the panel image), namely, their visually distorted bodies. As the comic continues across the page, and the boys walk through the hall of mirrors, different distortions occur through the mirror and in the panel images, and the panel sizes adapt to the perception of the boys. The point of view and focalization of the characters becomes that of the readers through the trick of the panel surfaces.

Comics narratology is of interest to you if you want to learn about:

- the telling of a tale and the processes involved in it, as well as the rendition of experience in perspective, focalization, and point of view;
- the distinction between the story and the discourse of a narrative, and how the discrepancies between them bring about narrative tension;
- the pacing and serialization of a comic's narrative.

Cognitive Approaches to Comics

Cognitive approaches to comics work with the mental processes that unfold as we read comics, make meaning from the lines and squiggles on the page, and construct their narratives. "Cognitive" refers here to all the possible mental involvements with the comics page: to the reasoned, (more) conscious process of inferencing, to the patterns of conceptual metaphors and to the embodied understanding of emotions, intentional stances, and movement. Charles Forceville (2005) has suggested that basic conceptual metaphors are visualized in comics, for example when Astérix is "steaming with anger." With a lobster-red face and puffs of steam coming out of his ears, the plucky little Gaul would be represented in a visual expression of the conceptual metaphor that "anger is a hot liquid in a container" (creating steam and pressure). The ways in which comics present complex constellations of "theory of mind," namely embedded assumptions about another's stance (meaning "he knows that I know that she plans"), has been considered by Lisa Zunshine (2011; see also Chapter 4). David Herman (2009) has outlined a more general account of comics narratives in the cognitive paradigm, and also much of my account of comics on these pages could be subsumed as "cognitive approaches to comics."

In the installment from *Little Nemo in Slumberland*, readers get a strongly embodied sense of the disorientation of "befuddlement hall." In the first panel, the characters have normal length. In the second panel, their upper bodies are stretched. In the third panel, their lower bodies are stretched. In the fourth panel, their entire bodies are stretched. Because images can affect your preconscious sense of your body, readers get an immediate impression of the irregular stretching processes at play here. In the second row of panels, the stretched body parts continue to be the same for all three boys, until the penultimate panel, where Nemo's body seems to contract, while the other two bodies stretch. Now the readers' body schema is entirely disoriented, and the confusion reaches its height. Through their embodied engagement, readers can experience the "befuddlement" of the three boys, as the comic toys with the representation of their bodies.

This cognitive approach to embodiment in the *Little Nemo* installment seems to be similar to the semiotic analysis I have outlined before. Taken in its widest possible sense, when semiotics is interested in meaning-making in general, there are a number of potential overlaps with cognitive approaches. Yet, whereas the semiotic approach relies on the relative sizes of the panels and their connection in an abstract, self-reliant system, the cognitive approach relates what we see on the page back to the meaning-making processes in the minds and bodies of readers. Cognitive approaches are based on results of empirical experiments of how we respond to texts and the world and generalize likely readerly involvement.

Cognitive approaches to comics are useful for you if you are interested in:

- how comics create meaning through cues and readerly inferences;
- how fictional minds and bodily experience are represented and elicited in comics.

Recommended Reading

Groensteen, Thierry. 2007. *The System of Comics*. Jackson: University of Mississippi Press.
Peeters, Benoît. 1991. *Case, planche, récit: lire la bande dessinée*. Paris: Casterman.
Magnussen, Anne. 2000. "The Semiotics of C.S. Peirce as a Framework for the Understanding of Comics." in Comics and Culture. Eds. Anne Magnussen and Hans-Christian Christiansen. Copenhagen: Museum Tusculanum Press. 193–207.

Groensteen and Peeters perhaps are the two most generally useful accounts of comics semiotics Magnussen combines the alternative semiotic tradition of C.S. Peirce with the study of comics.

Herman, David. 2009. *Basic Elements of Narrative*. Oxford: Wiley-Blackwell.

Chatman, Seymour. 1980. *Story and Discourse: Narrative Structure in Fiction and Film*. Ithaca: Cornell University Press.

Branigan, Edward. 1992. *Narrative Comprehension and Film*. London: Routledge.

Kukkonen, Karin. 2011. "Comics as a Testcase for Transmedial Narratology." *SubStance*, 40.1: 34–51.

David Herman outlines a basic, transmedial model of narrative, as does Chatman. While Herman relies largely on cognitive approaches to narrative, Chatman is rooted in the classical structuralist narratology, which is also represented by Genette (see Chapter 2). Branigan outlines the challenges which visual media pose to narratology. Kukkonen details the importance of the comics medium for the developing transmedial study of narrative.

Forceville, Charles. 2005. "Visual Representations of the Idealised Abstract Concept Model of Anger in the Asterix Album *La Zizanie*." *Journal of Pragmatics*, 37.1: 69–88.

Zunshine, Lisa. 2011. "What to Expect When You Pick Up A Graphic Novel." *SubStance*, 40.1: 114–34.

Johnson, Mark. 2007. *The Meaning of the Body: Aesthetics of Human Understanding*. Chicago: University of Chicago Press.

Forceville and Zunshine apply cognitive approaches to comics directly: Forceville applies (a version of) the conceptual metaphor theory; while Zunshine takes up theory of mind. Mark Johnson explores more general issues of embodiment and features a chapter on visual art.

Historical and Auteurist Approaches

So far, we have talked about the installment from *Little Nemo in Slumberland* as if it were a text freely floating in space and time. However, this comic was created by a particular author at a particular time and in a particular place, within a particular genre, under particular production conditions, and it is targeted at a particular audience. Considering the history of comics establishes the contexts of individual comics and ties them to the specific situation in time and space from which they emerge. This approach may relate comics to the historical events they represent or comment on in their narratives. We have already addressed how *Little Nemo* represents the city landscapes in the United States and the sense of wonder they can elicit at the turn of the twentieth century in Chapter 5. The approach may also write the history of a particular genre or character. In this section, I will briefly relate *Little Nemo in Slumberland* to

Winsor McCay himself as a comics author and to the historical context of writing for the Sunday pages.

Winsor McCay was not only a prolific author of comics, he was also a pioneer of animated film and a popular performer of so-called "chalk talks," a vaudeville act in which he would create and alter a drawing on a chalkboard while delivering a related monologue. In his animation film *Gertie the Dinosaur* (1914), McCay similarly interacts (himself on photographic film stock) with the animal he draws. In his earlier series *Tales of the Jungle Imps*, he illustrates just-so stories like "How The Turtle Got his Shell" (1903) or "How the Quillypig Got his Quills" (1903) by presenting readers with a series of images that show the changes in the animals. In his series *Dreams of the Rarebit Fiend*, McCay presents an adult dreamer whose dreams often draw on the basic parameters of the comic's creation, such as when the dreamer smears the ink he is drawn with as he moves, until the last panel is entirely black, or when the dreamer has to hold up the panel frames himself. The themes of metamorphosis, embodied movement, and the highlighting of the creative process can be traced across McCay's oeuvre and they form part of his distinctive vision for comics as an "auteur."

Little Nemo in Slumberland, like *Tales of the Jungle Imps*, was first published in the Sunday pages of the early twentieth-century newspapers. These Sunday pages were large and often reproduced in four-color print. They gave McCay ample space to develop his striking page layouts and sumptuous color compositions. The regular publication schedule fostered storytelling in installments (like *Little Nemo in Slumberland*) or in episodes relating to a similar theme (like *Tales of the Jungle Imps*). If you turn the pages in these Sunday newspapers, you will find other narratives, which relate cautionary tales or entertaining features on city life. Some of these more text-based newspaper formats were illustrated with images, and ornamental features will tie the paragraphs and images together to create a particular, dynamic page layout. The layout of the Sunday pages might well have contributed to McCay's eye for full-page mise en page, particularly in *Little Nemo*. This is not to say that McCay's *Little Nemo in Slumberland* was a predictable or inevitable event in the history of comics, but it highlights how closely related the series is to the context in which it was first published.

Consider historical and auteurist approaches to comics if you want to know more about:

- the production conditions under which comics were written;
- the audience for which a comic was originally written;
- their relation to other works of the author, or other contemporary cultural productions.

Cultural Studies and Gender Studies

Cultural Studies explores the connections between culture, power, and identity (see Marchart 2008). In John Frow's (1995) understanding, cultural studies relates any kind of text or cultural expression, such as comics, to the society from which they emerge and its value systems. It considers how a comic is inscribed in these value systems and the way the text reproduces them. In the tradition of Clifford Geertz (1993), cultural studies can also conceptualize stories and their communication as rituals: comics, as they constitute a social reality, enact and embody conflicts, and establish a sense of community and identity. Within this critical endeavor, gender studies focuses on the representation of gender differences in literature and the ideological implications of this.

Consider Little Nemo. He is by no means a "nobody," as his name suggests, but a young, white male. This might seem the normal choice for a comics hero. Cultural studies highlights how what we think is "normal" is in fact "normative," that is, perpetuating assumptions about what should be the case, and this we are not necessarily aware of. These tacit assumptions become more clear when we consider what Little Nemo is not. He is not a girl. In fact, there is a female character in Little Nemo, but she is simply called "the Princess" and her main importance for the series is to be the goal of Little Nemo's quest. Little Nemo is also not black or of a non-white ethnic origin. There is a black character in Little Nemo (you can seem him on the left in the installment we discussed), but he is represented as a cartoonish caricature, speaks in a childlike language, and is simply called "the Imp." As Winsor McCay posits a white male hero, he subscribes to and perpetuates the social values of his day; what Antonio Gramsci calls "hegemony." Cultural studies reveals these hidden political implications in comics.

Little Nemo in Slumberland can be seen as reflecting hegemony. It establishes the white male hero as a norm and desirable identity, and it constitutes a reality in which potential conflicts of interest between Nemo and the Imp, are obfuscated, as they both pursue the same quest and even are dressed in the same uniform. Yet the comic does not only pass value judgments but is also subject to them. As popular culture and recreational reading, *Little Nemo* does not confer much prestige to its readers. Pierre Bourdieu talks about "cultural capital" in this context: the more you know about socially valued culture, the more prestige you gather and the more opportunities you will find to acquire and display this cultural capital in social institutions. Broadly speaking, reading Shakespeare in school or seeing it performed in the theater, confers cultural capital on you. Reading *Little Nemo* does so to a much more limited extent.

However, the fact that you are reading this book means probably that you are studying comics at university or at least that you consider them worthy of serious critical attention. Bourdieu's account of "cultural capital" was written with the (French) bourgeois society of the twentieth century in mind, which valued a particular kind of education and culturedness. In the course of time, this valorization of high culture and bourgeois education might change again, redefining the cultural value systems and the sources of cultural capital.

Cultural Studies is worthwhile reading up on if you are interested in:

- the hidden political agendas of comics in terms of gender, social identities, and ethical relationships;
- the cultural role of comics, and their status in society.

Psychoanalysis

Like cultural studies is interested in hidden political agendas, in the same way psychoanalytical approaches are interested in the hidden psychological implications in texts and their place in the larger narrative of the development of the psyche they propose. Psychoanalytical approaches to comics are perhaps most common in French comics criticism (see Ann Miller 2007 for an overview), but they have also gathered importance in the discussion of autobiographical comics such as *Maus* and their treatment of trauma.

This installment (fig. 6.2) shows Little Nemo descending into the "world of wonderful dreams" and travelling through a mushroom forest, until he characteristically wakes up again in the real world in the last panel. We could read this installment as an illustration of Sigmund Freud's ideas about dreams, the unconscious and the repressed. According to Freud's *Interpretation of Dreams* (1999; first published 1899), our dreams give us access to our unconscious in which everything we repress in our waking life is collected. We lose control over our rational minds in the unconscious, and when the repressed returns, we are often incapable of controlling it. Little Nemo in this installment could be seen as descending into his unconscious. According to Freud, dreams work through condensation and displacement; they do not give a literal representation of our problems but turn the issues we are troubled by into metaphors and images. Little Nemo's helplessness in the mushroom hall can be read as a condensed and displaced representation of an encounter with the unconscious. As he leans against the fragile structure of his mental world, Nemo loses his footing and gets whisked away, almost drowning in the mushrooms. Some editions of Freud's *Interpretation of*

Figure 6.2 Little Nemo (III). (1905). *Source:* SFCGA - San Francisco Academy of Comic Art Collection, The Ohio State University Billy Ireland Cartoon Library and Museum.

Dreams reproduce a comics page by the psychoanalyst Sandor Ferenczi, depicting a metamorphosis not dissimilar to *Little Nemo in Slumberland*, as an illustration of condensation and displacement (see Peeters 1991, 22–3). Strikingly, Freud had used the mushroom metaphor himself in his *Interpretation of Dreams* to describe the "dream wish," which emerges from the web of our (unconscious) thoughts "like a mushroom from its mycelium" (1999, 341).

An alternative psychoanalytical account to Freud's is that of the French psycho-analyst Jacques Lacan. Lacan distinguishes between three phases of human development: the order of the real (in which we follow our biological needs), the imaginary order (better known as the "mirror phase," in which we desire the mother) and the symbolic order (in which we are inscribed into a social order). The symbolic order is patriarchal; it is based on the "name of the father," which outlines its rules and interdictions. When Little Nemo wakes up in the final panel, he is immediately reinscribed into the social order with his father present and uttering an interdiction. Note the similarities between the clown Komoko in the dreamworld, who tells him not to touch the mushrooms, and Nemo's father in the last panel: also in the dreamworld, the "name of the father" and the rule-bound world he stands for, are present. Transgressing these rules creates chaos and fear in Little Nemo, and he calls out for the security and order of his "home" and "Papa."

The encounter with the unconscious or the ordering power of the "name of the father" are only small sections of the complex psychoanalytical theory models of Freud and Lacan. More generally, psychoanalytical accounts of comics are of interest to you if you want to investigate:

- how comics represent fears and desires;
- why comics might leave out certain elements from their narrative, and how these gaps can be related to the unconscious;
- how psychoanalysis, a dominant mode of thinking in the twentieth-century, left its traces in comics narratives.

Recommended Reading

Sabin, Roger. 1993. *Adult Comics: An Introduction*. London: Routledge.

Witek, James. 1986. *Comic Books as History: The Narrative Art of Jack Jackson, Art Spiegelman and Harvey Pekar*. Jackson: University Press of Mississippi.

Gabilliet, Jean-Paul. 2010. *Of Comics and Men: A Cultural History of American Comic Books*. Translated by Bart Beaty and Paul Nguyen. Jackson: University of Mississippi Press.

Sabin, Witek, and Gabilliet present three historical approaches to comics with different emphases. Sabin addresses the importance of the historical context of the 1980s for the development of what he calls "adult comics." Witek discusses the representation of history in comics, and Gabilliet offers a history of US comics across the twentieth century.

Geertz, Clifford. 1993. *The Interpretation of Cultures*. London: Fontana. Ch.15. Deep Play: Notes on the Balinese Cockfight.

Bourdieu, Pierre. 2011. *Distinction: A Social Critique of the Judgement of Taste*. Routledge Classics. London: Routledge.

Geertz's interpretation of a cockfight in Bali shows how this ritualistic event throws social realities into relief, and how it plays out social roles and identities. Geertz compares the event throughout the essay to the way in which novels (and arguably, comics) work in a cultural community. Bourdieu provides a sociological analysis of cultural value systems implicit in "taste" and the prestige that goes with it.

Freud, Sigmund. 1999. *The Interpretation of Dreams*. Oxford Classics. Oxford: Oxford University Press.

Žižek, Slavoj. 1991. *Looking Awry: An Introduction to Jacques Lacan through Popular Culture*. Cambridge, MA: MIT Press.

Miller, Ann. 2007. *Reading Bande Dessinée: Critical Approaches to French Language Comic Strip*. Bristol: Intellect. Ch.11. Psychoanalytic Approaches to Tintin.

Freud and Žižek offer introductions to the respective psychoanalytical theories of Freud and Lacan. Žižek applies different aspects of Lacan's theory to film and popular culture in accessible language. Miller's account shows how psychoanalytical approaches were used (in different ways) to shed light on comics in particular. Miller focuses on French comics, but offers a useful general introduction to the issues at stake and the research literature.

References

Branigan, Edward. 1992. *Narrative Comprehension and Film*. London: Routledge.

Chatman, Seymour. 1980. *Story and Discourse: Narrative Structure in Fiction and Film*. Ithaca: Cornell University Press.

Forceville, Charles. 2005. "Visual Representations of the Idealised Abstract Concept Model of Anger in the Asterix Album *La Zizanie*." *Journal of Pragmatics*, 37.1: 69–88.

Freud, Sigmund. 1999. *The Interpretation of Dreams*. Oxford Classics. Oxford: Oxford University Press.

Frow, Jonathan. 1995. *Cultural Studies and Cultural Value*. Oxford: Oxford University Press.

Groensteen, Thierry. 2007. *The System of Comics*. Jackson: University of Mississippi Press.

Herman, David. 2009. *Basic Elements of Narrative*. Oxford: Wiley-Blackwell.

Marchart, Oliver. 2008. *Cultural Studies*. Konstanz: UVK Verlagsgesellschaft.

Peeters, Benoît. 1991. *Case, planche, récit: Lire la bande dessinée*. Paris: Casterman.

Zunshine, Lisa. 2011. "What to Expect When You Pick Up A Graphic Novel." *SubStance*, 40.1: 114–34.

* * *

My introductions to each of these critical approaches to comics has been very short, and my readings of *Little Nemo in Slumberland* through them are only rough sketches of the kinds of interpretations these approaches can provide and the kinds of questions they can answer. This section is meant to give you an idea of the work possible through some of the academic disciplines from which comics have been approached. There are others, like art history or media studies, which have not been introduced here but touched on elsewhere in this book. As I said in the beginning, comics studies has a wide array of disciplines to draw on for discussing comics, and what you will hopefully take away from this overview is some idea of how these approaches work and how they can be combined to provide a richer account of what comics are.

Class Activity 6: Comics Criticism

Choose a comic which has been published in the last six month and start a web search on what critical reviews it has received. Discuss the reviews you find in your group. Where have the reviews been published? What do the reviews discuss? What do they consider as important? What kinds of things do they mention what kinds of things do they ignore? Why do you think the reviews were written?

Class Activity 7: Time Travel in the Archive

Have a look at the "cartoon image database" of the Billy Ireland Cartoon Library (cartoons.osu.edu). Search in "advanced search" for all comics and cartoons that were published in the year your (great-) grandfather or grandmother was born. Browse through your search result and compare (some of) them to the comics you are familiar with. What has changed in drawing styles, page layout, and panel design? What has remained the same? Do you recognize any names, characters, or themes? How would you find out more about them?

Writing Assignment 6

Take the first of your writing assignments and identify the critical approaches you have brought to bear on the comic there. Select two more approaches from the ones described here and analyze that comic again through these approaches. How does your analysis change? What new conclusions have you drawn? How can they be combined with your previous conclusions? Please write 300–500 words.

How to Write Your Essay on Comics

If you are reading this book as part of a class on comics, you probably have to write a critical essay, investigating an issue to do with comics and unfolding a coherent argument about it. The suggested essay topics at the end of each chapter provide you with some idea of what essay topics in the field of comics studies could look like. Each of the essay topics addresses particular instances in the comics text and connects them to a larger issue, such as realism (for *Blankets*) or popular culture (for *Watchmen*). On the basis of textual evidence and what you have read from other critics, you will then develop your own argument about the issue and present it in your essay. Your teacher can advise you on how to do this in your individual essay project. These are some general suggestions and observations on writing essays on comics.

Consider your essay project as the work of a detective. You encounter a particular scene of evidence; you investigate how one element relates to another; you interrogate witnesses; you develop an argument about how it all connects, and you present this argument to your audience in the final parlor room scene.

Figure 6.3 Promethea. *Source:* from *Promethea, Book 3* © DC Comics. Used with Permission.

Figure 6.3 (Cont'd) Promethea. Source: from Promethea, Book 3 © DC Comics. Used with Permission.

This is a rough analogy, of course, but it might help you make sense of what you are doing in a research essay and understand how it can be fun at times. Let's go through the process step by step.

The Crime Scene

Consider the comic you are working with as your crime scene. Here you can find the first batch of evidence to make your case. You might have been assigned this particular comic in your essay topic, you might have chosen it yourself, or you might have selected it because it connects with a more general essay topic you might have been given. In any case, it pays to examine your textual evidence closely before you go any further.

Keep notes as you read through your comic. Write down which pages attract your attention. Is it because they stand out in a particular way? Is it because they show patterns of repetition? Is it because the written text features a striking quote? These are the pages you will want to come back to when you select passages from the comic to support your argument. There is no standard protocol for taking notes from a comic, but you might find the suggestions in the "Annotations" helpful. The categories for the annotations are based on the checklists from Chapters 1 and 2.

The Witnesses

After you have investigated your comic and ordered the textual evidence in your annotations, it is time to find other opinions and gain a broader perspective on the case. There are different kinds of witnesses you might want to consult: encyclopedias and dictionaries; critical writing on the comics you read; academic sources on the more general topics you address. Reading for an essay tends to be an unpredictable process, and you might move back and forth between different sources (just like a detective who checks back with his witnesses time and again). It might be a good idea to start with the most specific of witnesses and work your way to the more general. For example, read up on critical writing (both in reviews and in academic criticism) and research what others have said about this particular comic. Do they observe the same things about the comic? Do you agree with their interpretation? Do you disagree (and on what textual evidence do you base this disagreement)? Select topics and themes, which you have observed in the comic itself or which other critics have highlighted in their reviews and articles, and then go on to consult the more general research, for example on "endless loops" or

---

Box 6.1   *Annotations for Figure 6.3*

Page layout:	six panels; vertical gutters; even distribution across the page; continuous background.
Characters and events:	Sophie and Barbara in conversation; continuous movement.
Gaze direction:	along the Moebius strip; top left → bottom right → top right → bottom left → top left (circular); tied to the character's displacement across the page.
Storyworld:	Moebius strip in the foreground; not anchored in the background; celestial bodies; Egyptian pyramids and obelisks.
Composition:	strikingly symmetrical, but details destabilize this, such as the positions of the characters on the Moebius strip and smaller features of the path itself.
Visual style:	ligne claire; reminds me of the work of Moebius (Jean Giraud).
Dialogue:	characters talk about being on a "Moebius strip" and being in a time loop; no discernible beginning and end points.
Key terms:	"intricate"; "insane"; "infinity"; "madness"; "reason."
Position in the barrative:	mid-point in Promethea's quest through the realm of reason; crisis of the quest (resolved on the next page).

Narration / focalization / point of view:

No discernible narrator; focalization of the two women (through looping gaze direction and dialogue), exterior, distanced point of view; long shot; each of the panels taken individually has a slightly changing perspective to reflect the changing relating between the characters and the Moebius strip.

In order to ascertain the effects of certain features of the page, play through possible alternative versions. What if the panels were arranged in a straight line, rather than on the page? Would this change the characters' movement and relation to each other? What if the size and angle of the images were different? What if you only read the speech bubbles and captions without the images? As you compile your annotations, quite often a pattern is emerging that cuts across categories, and that could form the point of departure for your analysis (such as the Moebius-strip in this example). You will find a more fully developed analysis of this double page in the conclusion. Not everything you will find on a page will fit the categories above. Write additional notes to record anything that strikes, intrigues and puzzles you – chances are it will become relevant for your analysis. Write down words or ideas you are not sure about and look them up later. Even though the categories above do not cover all possible observations, if you keep your notes consistently in this format, it will be easy to make comparisons between different pages of the same comic and between different comics.

Moebius patterns in literature look up "Moebius strip" in an encyclopedia and learn more about where the term comes from, how it is used, and what it describes. Again you should take notes to keep track of what you learn from these witnesses.

As a good detective, you should be suspicious of your witnesses. Most texts have their own agenda. They present their argument from a certain perspective, support it through rhetorical strategies, and attempt to guide their readers. This is a perfectly legitimate strategy, and I will suggest you do the same when you write your essay, but it is important to keep the agenda of a text in mind when you read it yourself. As part of your investigation, you should keep track of the interests and rhetorical strategies of the texts you are working with. Do they write from the vantage point of one or more of the critical approaches to comics I have outlined in this chapter? Which passages from the comic have they chosen to support their argument? Which have they omitted? How have they arranged the steps of their argument to make their conclusion salient? Be respectful to the sources you consult, and reference them, but do not feel obliged to accept what they say to be the last and final word.

Making Your Case

Your witnesses cannot have the last and final word, because it is you who will set them up side by side and contrast their statements with your own observations – at least in the framework of your essay. At this stage of your essay project, you should have a copious set of notes from your primary and your secondary reading. Think about the argument you would like to make. Which passages from the comic can illustrate it? Which critical assessments of the comic or the topic at large can support it? Which contradict it? How would you answer these challenges? It might be useful to write down individual points on Post-it notes and keep rearranging them until they form a structure that makes sense to you. Give yourself time to figure out the plan for your essay. After all, most detectives struggle to make sense of their cases. Go back to the comic or the secondary reading for inspiration or let your plan rest for a couple days before you work on it again.

Once you have a good sense of what you will argue, start writing. It is now time to arrange your evidence to the best effect and relevance, and to set up the finale of your essay project: your parlor room scene. At the end of a detective novel or film, the investigator will assemble all the witnesses, assess all the evidence and solve the case. Your essay should be similar to this final parlor room scene. Here, you present your case, the problem, or question you have researched, and the conclusions you came to. Like any good detective, you need to support your conclusions with evidence (from the primary text) and with the corroborating statements of witnesses (from your secondary reading). Get readers hooked with a striking introduction, make sure you ask the right questions to keep their attention and present evidence that will lead them to the conclusion. Sherlock Holmes and Hercule Poirot might make this look easy, but a good parlor room scene needs to be carefully constructed and meticulously rehearsed, so that you achieve the right arc of attention and the right turn of phrase. Draft and redraft your essay until it seems just right.

Revising your essay is important to give it that "easy" finish. Poirot in the TV show has only a limited amount of time to solve his case and present his evidence in the parlor room scene; similarly, you have an essay deadline to meet and only a limited number of pages for your essay. Give yourself enough time for revisions and use them well to shape your essay so that it can make its point in the allotted number of pages. First and foremost, you need to convince your readers in your parlor room scene. But you also need to use a style of writing and argument that is appropriate for your subject. Ask your teacher to explain what is expected if you are uncertain about this. More generally, make sure that your writing allows for smooth reading with grammatical accuracy and no spelling mistakes. There are many guides to writing that can help you with this.

End Credits

At the end of your paper, the credits start rolling. You need to list all your sources, primary and secondary, in a section called "Works Cited." The Works Cited section makes your references traceable and is thus the basis of your academic accountability – one of the most important features of the textual detective. The citation conventions below are based on the MLA Style, in my opinion the most convenient style for referencing comics. Your teacher might have a preferred convention for referencing or perhaps a style sheet of their own for you. Generally, it is important to be consistent in your referencing.

Based on the MLA Citation convention, parenthesis style, you can cite comics as follows:

- for a comic book: (Writer Page number) as a parenthetic reference in the text, for example (Azzarello 12).

   In the Works Cited section: Azzarello, Brian, writer. "Parlez Kung Vous" *100 Bullets*. Illus. Eduardo Risso. New York, DC Comics, 2000.
- for a single volume trade paperback: (Writer Page number) as a parenthetic reference in the text, for example (Moore 12).

   In the Works Cited section: Moore, Alan, writer. *Watchmen*. Illus. Dave Gibbons. Colors by Anthony Higgins. New York: DC Comics, 1986.
- for a multivolume trade paperback: (Writer Volume: Page number) as a parenthetic reference in the text, for example (Ellis 2:12).

   In the Works Cited section: Ellis, Warren, writer. *Planetary*. Illus. John Cassaday. Colors by Laura Depuy. 3 vols. New York: Wildstorm, 1999–2009.
- for a multivolume trade paperback, which is not paginated: (Writer Volume: Issue: Page number) as a parenthetic reference in the text, for example (Moore 2:7:12).

   In the Works Cited section: Moore, Alan, writer. *Promethea*. Illus. J.H. Williams III. et al. 5 vols. La Jolla, CA: ABC Comics, 1999–2005.

You should add a footnote whenever you count pages to reference an unpaginated comic book or trade paperback and explain that you have done so.

Recommended Reading

Creme, Phyllis and Mary R. Lea. 2002. *Writing At University: A Guide for Students.* Buckingham and Philadelphia: Open University Press.

MLA Handbook for Writers of Research Papers. 2009. 7th edition. New York: The Modern Language Association of America.

Based on their own research, Creme and Lea offer guidance on how to gain academic literacy and write essays in the style that is expected, in particular if you are not used to writing at university. The *MLA Handbook* provides you with everything you need to know about citing comics and critical literature in MLA Style, and offers plenty of information on research methods and the mechanics of writing.

There is no essay question connected to this chapter but some recommendations on how to write your essay on comics.

Conclusion

Comics as Literature

It is quite rare for textbooks to have a conclusion. After all, textbooks open a new territory for students and equip them to master its heights and pitfalls themselves. Textbooks are not supposed to tell the end of the story. This book has looked at comics from many different angles: comics as a medium of popular culture which develops a stake in the more general cultural debate; comics as part of convergence culture and intermedial exchange; and comics as complex texts which need careful attention in their analysis. In this conclusion, I would like to trace one way which the study of comics can take from here: considering comics as literature. There are many other ways you might choose, and this certainly not the end of the story.

Comics are different from the prose texts commonly considered "literature." They use not only words but also images, and the lettering and layout of comics is much more important than in books. Still, comics are not entirely dissimilar from traditional books: they tell stories, both highly fictitious and agonizingly authentic; they spin metaphors and entangle us in cognitive complexities; they take us into fantastic storyworlds and let us see the special moments in the most mundane of existences. Comics can be every bit as complicated, engaging, and enchanting as novels, and I argue that they should be analyzed on the same footing in literary study. For this, *Studying Comics and Graphic Novels* advocates thinking of what we see on the page in terms of clues and inferences, because such an approach allows us to trace our multifold interactions with the page in front of us, the complexity of drafting and redrafting inferences, and the multiple possible paths we can take across the page. Such an understanding of

Studying Comics and Graphic Novels, First Edition. Karin Kukkonen.
© 2013 John Wiley & Sons, Ltd. Published 2013 by John Wiley & Sons, Ltd.

comics provides an interface between comics studies and the close reading of literary criticism, bringing literary approaches to bear on comics texts. Not every comic will sustain the weight of literary analysis, but then not every novel, poem, or play will either.

In 1943, William Marston, the author of *Wonder Woman*, wrote an article in *American Scholar*, in which he claims that "100,000,000 Americans" cannot be wrong in reading comics because the medium "plays a trite but lusty tune on the C natural keys of human nature" (36). According to Marston, comics engage our emotional responses and our deepest wishes, and that is a fair enough reason to grant them cultural relevance. Marston's article drew a response from Cleanth Brooks and Robert Heilman in the next issue of the journal. Brooks and Heilman, who would both go on to become famous literary critics, conclude their response sarcastically by suggesting giving up on the written word and its complexities and to "bring the power of the 'visual image' to the aid of puny reason" (1943, 252; see Gardner 2012, 82–4 for a more detailed discussion of this exchange). Brooks and Heilman ridicule Marston's optimistic belief in images and emotions as a force for the greater good and his seemingly unreflected use of language. Even if Brooks, the father of close reading, capitulates when faced with images, and does not even consider the possibility of the textual analysis of comics, we don't have to lay down our arms with him. Comics studies today has moved on from the reductive positions of either Marston (who reduces the immediate, embodied qualities of comics to a trigger of primordial pleasures) or Brooks and Heilman (who deny comics any complexity or intellectual challenge) and can consider comics as a literary form.

At first glance, this double page from Alan Moore and J.H. Williams III's *Promethea* (Figure 6.3, p.140–1) seems very orderly. It is partitioned into six lengthy panels, and the horizon in the background then halves each of these panels once more. However, this horizon is somewhat peculiar: the pyramids and the obelisks of the upper half of the page are seemingly reflected on the surface of the lower half. Still this inference has to be qualified, because while we can read the surface around the line of the horizon as a reflecting pool of water, once our gaze roams below, we see a sky with stars, and the surface suddenly reads as clouds or mist. There is a strong, and pleasing, symmetry on this double page, but it is not easily resolved into a surface reflection, which would allow us to relate all elements to each other. The sun in the middle of the top row of panels could be seen as reflected in the round shape in the middle of the bottom row of panels, but this reflection is in fact the moon, a celestial body in its own right. This ambiguity makes it hard for readers to get a stable sense of what they see and a clear orientation on the page. If we as readers can rationalize the inversion of the top and bottom half of the page as a reflection, it does not disturb our body schema (and presumably that's perhaps why our first inference would be the reflection). If we read it as a nightly realm, similar but ontologically different from the sunny realm above, however, then we have a problem: everything is upside down in the lower half of the page. Just as with the Rubin vase (Figure 1.4), we can only grasp and orient ourselves with regard to one half of the page at a time.

The path on which the two women walk has the shape of a Moebius strip: an endless path which, even though it loops, only has one surface to tread on. As the women progress along the path, they move through the sunny realm and through the nightly realm, and they walk on top of the path and then below it, but in fact, they never get anywhere. If we just go by the representation of their bodies, the two women hardly seem to move a muscle for their walking. If this were a panel sequence in a single row, it would seem as if they scarcely moved at all. If the landscape in the background of this (imagined) panel sequence were continuous, as in the actual page, it would seem as if the women floated across the face of the earth. On the actual page, we see the women at different points in time, broken by the gutters, and understand that they must have moved from one panel to another. Yet, even though they change their position along the continuous image, their lack of movement makes them seem to stand still at the same time as they make their way across the Moebius strip.

Nevertheless, these two women seem to affect our body schema strongly. The reason for this is that, as we scan the page from the left to the right, we become slowly aware that they are actually walking both on the upper and on the lower surface of the strip in the same panels. On the left-hand side, we can almost ignore this information, because the path itself partly covers what is beneath. Especially if we don't read the speech bubbles yet, we perhaps won't notice that anything is amiss for the moment. On the right-hand side, however, we are then confronted in the fourth panel with the two women walking upside down. This deeply disrupting, because, first, our body schema and the attendant sense of gravity tells us that the lower couple should simply fall off, and because, second, they are in two places at the same time, both above and below. Just as we have noted for the entire composition of the page, what might be perceived as symmetry at first suddenly becomes disturbing.

What we experience from the form of this page, the way the panels are arranged and the way the bodies of the women move across its surface, contributes to the larger conceptual discussion which is at stake in this instance in the comic, namely reason and its inversions. Brooks and Heilman see language-based reason, symmetric and well-ordered, as the obvious choice for making sense. This double page, however, demonstrates how such rational symmetry can not only be evoked by images but also suddenly turn into madness and repression when the screw is turned too far. The page presents an ordered and accessible layout at first glance, pleasing to our body schema because of its vertical and horizontal doublings. Once we have a closer look, however, these doublings begin to disturb us. The storyworld cannot be processed coherently; gravity is disabled and bodies are in two places at the same time. Grasping this double page in readers' embodied meaning-making seems to be always in reach and is yet constantly prevented. At the same time, the two women seem to glide across the page, travelling without moving, as if nothing were amiss, yet never able to develop any traction on the path.

The dialogue in the speech bubbles makes it obvious that the characters are already in their second tour around the loop. The first panel is both the first panel on the page and a continuation from the last panel, just below, and the inescapability of the loop becomes clear when we see the question "how do we get off this thing?" in the last panel, only to continue reading from the first panel all over again. Just as the characters in the storyworld cannot find a way off the Moebius strip, so the mise en page does not offer readers any way off the comics page. What we see on this double page seems to fall neatly into the categories of past, present and future, but actually transcends them. The gliding motion of the women underlines that they are never rooted at a point in time. At the same time, the dialogue between the two women works itself as an endless loop and addresses the concept of the Moebius strip. Just as the two women are walking on the path and pointing to their own previous (and consecutive) selves in the images, so the language of the dialogue and the topic it refers to reflect each other. A clear delineation of usually distinct categories, such as past-present-future or signifier-signified, becomes all but impossible.

How can we integrate these three levels of observation (composition, the characters' bodies and their discourse), which roughly corresponds to the three constitutive features of comics (sequence, image, and word), into a common framework?

Both cognitive psychology and literary theory can help us here. The psychologist Lawrence Barsalou (2008) suggests that we think through concepts not in terms of an abstract generalized description stored in our brain, but rather in terms of a set of instructions cueing us to run a simulation of encountering the object, of experiencing it. While Barsalou's basic argument refers to the concepts we have of concrete objects, such as "table," or simple emotions, such as "anger," it can arguably be extended to the representation of more complex concepts in literature as well. The double page from *Promethea* offers readers a set of clues, which prompts them to run a simulation of the conceptual issue at stake. The slippage between reason and madness, the dark underbelly of a well-ordered worldview, is experienced by readers since symmetry cannot be processed in a coherent fashion and because a double pull of gravity disrupts how we relate the bodies of characters, seemingly at ease, through our body schema. The continuous dialogue in the speech bubbles and the continuous movement of the characters along the Moebius strip reinforce the sense of inescapability from this precarious and uncanny condition. It all seems to make perfect sense until it doesn't.

Barsalou calls his take on concepts "situated conceptualization." According to this model, we create a simulation of what it is like to interact with the concepts in our minds, and of what it is like "being there" in a situation that involves them. The double page from *Promethea* creates such a "situated conceptualization." In the terms of literary criticism, we could say that it works in some ways like an "objective correlative" of the precariousness and uncanniness of reason. "Objective correlative" is a term coined by T.S. Eliot, author of *The Wasteland* and himself an avid comics reader (see Chinitz 2003). "Objective correlative," in Eliot's definition, refers to "a set of objects, a situation, a chain of events which shall be the formula of that *particular* emotion; such that when the external facts, which must terminate in sensory experience, are given, the emotion is immediately evoked" (1972, 100). What we see on a comics page, the situation and the events which it represents, gives rise to a specific and well-controlled emotional experience. From the cognitive angle of Barsalou, the ways in which this page elicits a "situated conceptualization" relies similarly on a "sensory experience," and the page not only leads to an emotional experience but also prompt its readers to think through conceptual issues. The form of the page, that is, the particular ways in which it manipulates what we expect of page layout, dialogue, and character movement in comics, creates readerly experience and establishes connections to a larger conceptual issue.

Promethea perhaps belongs to what Matthew Arnold calls "the best that has been thought and written" on the human imagination and our cognitive and embodied encounter with the world, on our uses of language and our experience through it. The comic gives new perspectives on the importance of the imagination for our thinking, on how the imagination relates to our other mental capacities and on how human beings engage with it in literary and creative processes. *Promethea*, which draws on the *Wonder Woman* comics that sparked the debate between Marston, Brooks, and Heilman seventy years ago, uses the emotional power of images to achieve reasoned complexity.

The purpose of this analysis of *Promethea* is not to provide proof that comics can be literary (though if any reader has found it at this point in the book,

I shall be glad). Rather, it serves as an example of how a literary analysis of a comic based on the framework of *Studying Comics and Graphic Novels* could proceed. Of course, this analysis would need to be extended to the entire series; it would need to enter a conversation with previous critical discussions of these pages and be contextualized in the cultural environment that Moore and Williams draw on. This analysis (and this book in general) are only a small part of the much larger endeavor of bringing comics into literary studies, of moving beyond the juxtaposition of the powers of images and words, and this endeavor is far from being concluded.

References

Barsalou, Lawrence. 2008. "Situating Concepts." In *The Cambridge Handbook of Situated Cognition*, edited by Philip Robbins and Murat Ayede, 236–63. Cambridge: Cambridge University Press.

Brooks, Cleanth and Robert Heilman. 1943. "To the Editor." *American Scholar*, 13.2: 248–52.

Chinitz, David. 2003. *T.S. Eliot and the Cultural Divide*. Chicago: University of Chicago Press.

Eliot, T.S. 1972. *The Sacred Wood: Essays on Poetry and Criticism*. London: Methuen.

Gardner, Jared. 2012. *Projections: Comics and the History of Twenty-First Century Storytelling*. Stanford: Stanford University Press.

Marston, William Moulston. 1943. "Why 100,000,000 Americans Read Comics." *American Scholar*, 13.1: 35–44.

Appendix: More Comics and Graphic Novels to Read

This section features brief outlines of individual comics and graphic novels, some of which have been discussed before in this book, and some of which are reading suggestions. The selection goes beyond English-language comics and collects some of the most talked-about texts, yet it is certainly not comprehensive. It is mainly intended as a starting point for you to discover more reading material. For a much more extended list, consult *1001 Comics You Must Read Before You Die*, edited by Paul Gravette (Quintessence Editions, 2011).

100 Bullets (1999–2009). Writer: Brian Azzarello. Illustrator: Eduardo Risso. Vertigo / DC

Running through 100 issues, *100 Bullets* takes readers into a noirish storyworld. Agent Graves approaches people who have been wronged in life and offers them 100 untraceable bullets to set the grievance right. Their moral decisions are embedded in the conspiracy of the Trust, the twelve families that actually run the United States. Azzarello's narrative and Risso's complex mise en pages present the entanglements of the characters with each other and their attempts to find their ways through the labyrinthine and threatening storyworld.

American Splendor (1976–2008). Writer: Harvey Pekar. Illustrators: Daniel Haspiel, Frank Stack et al. DC Comics

American Splendor is a series of autobiographical comics by writer Harvey Pekar, who reflects on his life and personal anxieties in the contemporary United States. Recent collections of this series include *The Quitter* (illustrated by Daniel Haspiel), chronicling episodes of Pekar's youth and adolescence,

Studying Comics and Graphic Novels, First Edition. Karin Kukkonen.
© 2013 John Wiley & Sons, Ltd. Published 2013 by John Wiley & Sons, Ltd.

and *Our Cancer Year* (authored together with his wife Joyce Brabner and illustrated by Frank Stack).

Animal Man (1988–90). Writer: Grant Morrison. Illustrators: Chaz Truog and Doug Hazlewood. DC Comics

When DC relaunched the superhero Animal Man in 1988, writer Grant Morrison chose to present his adventures in a highly self-reflexive and politically aware fashion. After various adventures with species-related powers, Morrison himself makes an appearance in Animal Man's (metafictional) quest to meet his creator and question his right to intervene in his life.

Bad Machinery (2009–). Writer and Illustrator: John Allison. Web

Bad Machinery is a web comic which chronicles the adventures of a group of schoolchildren. These adventures, which stretch across several installments, could be described as Enid-Blytonesque but are told with a pleasantly dry sense of humor.

Batman: Dark Knight Returns (1986). Writer and Illustrator: Frank Miller. DC Comics

Perhaps the most famous of all Batman comics, Frank Miller's version brings the masculine anxieties of Batman to the fore. Together with his (now female) side-kick Robyn, Batman comes from retirement to rid Gotham City once and for all from evil. Miller's angry, nervous drawing style and the pain and punishment inflicted on Batman (and the other superheroes) make *Dark Knight Returns* one of the key examples of the deconstruction of the superhero in the late 1980s.

Batman: The Killing Joke (1988). Writer: Alan Moore. Illustrator: Brian Boland. DC Comics

This Batman story retells the original story of the Joker. Alan Moore gives the character depth, as he investigates the despair and disappointment that underlies the psychosis of the villain.

Binky Brown meets the Holy Virgin Mary (1972). Writer and Illustrator: Justin Green. McSweeney's (new edition)

One of the earliest autobiographical comics, emerging out of the underground movement, *Binky Brown* renders Green's experiences of a Catholic education in a highly expressive and explicit style. Art Spiegelman hails *Binky Brown* in his foreword as the comic that made *Maus* "possible."

Blankets (2003). Writer and Illustrator: Craig Thompson. Top Shelf Productions

Craig Thompson's autobiographical comic tells of his growing up in Michigan, his experiences with Evangelical Christianity, and his first love. The comic attracted mainstream comics awards, like the Eisner Award for Best Writer in 2004, which are rarely given to autobiographical comics, and enjoys popularity across the alternative comics spectrum.

Cerebus the Aardvark (1977–2004). Writer and Illustrator: Dave Sim. Aardvark-Vanaheim

The key example for an independent comic, self-published (at first) yet still produced on a regular schedule, *Cerebus the Aardvark* is one of the longest-running comics narratives. It takes its author, and readers, from a fantasy adventure into political commentary and autobiographical narrative as it unfolds over several thousand pages and 300 issues.

City of Glass: The Graphic Novel (1994). Writers: Paul Auster and Paul Karasik. Illustrator: Dave Mazzucchelli. Avon Books / Picador

Adapting the novel *City of Glass* by Paul Auster, the comic by Mazzucchelli and Karasik unfolds a narrative that leads its protagonist through many embedded stories and throws him back onto to himself through self-reflexive loops. The comic renders a highly complex narrative in and about language visually in images and mise en page.

Classics Illustrated: Wuthering Heights (1949/2009). Illustrator: Henry C. Kiefer. Classics Illustrated

The Classics Illustrated adaptation of Emily Brontë's novel *Wuthering Heights*. Classics Illustrated has adopted a wide range of what can be considered "literary classics."

A Contract with God and Other Tenement Stories (1978). Writer and Illustrator: Will Eisner. Baronet / DC Comics

The first graphic novel to go by this name, *A Contract with God* shows the more serious side of Will Eisner. The comic collects four connected short stories, all set in the same housing area in New York. Other graphic novels by Eisner written in this vein are *The Building, Dropsie Avenue*, and *To The Heart of the Storm*.

Crisis on Infinite Earths (1985). Writer: Marv Wolfman. Illustrator: George Pérez. DC Comics

Crisis on Infinite Earths presents the DC multiverse and its cataclysm. Alternative versions of the superheroes are located in the alternative worlds of the DC multiverse: there are "earths" on which Superman has married Lois Lane and on which Lex Luthor is the hero. In this story, which engages self-reflexively with this superhero trope, the alternative earths begin to collapse, and the DC multiverse develops towards a universe again.

The Complete Crumb Comics. Writer and Illustrator: Robert Crumb. A seventeen-volume collection of Crumb's work, published by Fantagraphic Comics (1987–2005)

This collection brings together Crumb's varied oeuvre, featuring comics such as *Fritz the Cat* and reprints of from Crumb's *Zap!* and *Weirdo* magazines. If you want to know more about Crumb and his work, his web page (rcrumb.com) is also worth a visit.

Desolation Jones (2005–7). Writer: Warren Ellis. Illustrator: J.H. Williams III et al. Wildstorm

In a bad-future Los Angeles, the discarded MI5 agent Jones tries to make a fresh start. However, this is not to be as he finds himself in the basic plot of Raymond Chandler's *The Big Sleep*, and gets caught up a noirish nightmare involving a degenerate rich family, body-modified secret agents, and life-threatening mysteries.

Donald Duck (1937–). Writers and Illustrators: Carl Barks, Don Rosa et al. Various editions in several languages

Donald Duck is a long-running series of comic books chronicling the adventures of Donald and his family in Duckburg and throughout the world. Carl Barks, who drew the series from 1943, displays a keen sense of presenting actions and events in a clean, clear drawing style, and he has significantly shaped the looks of Donald Duck. Don Rosa, who took up Donald Duck comics in the 1990s, uses a more careful and detailed drawing style and often presents local settings with an ironic twist. Popular Don Rosa stories are *The Life and Times of Scrooge McDuck* and *The Quest for Kalevala* (*Sammon salaisuus*).

The EC Archives (2006–8). Various Writers and Illustrators. Gemstone Publishing

A series of reprints from the original EC comic books of the 1940s and 1950s, such as *Tales from The Crypt*, *Vault of Horror*, *Crime SuspenStories* and others.

Epileptic (1996). Writer and Illustrator: David B. Jonathan Cape

David B's autobiographic comic about life as an epileptic renders the author's personal experience in a highly expressive drawing style and through innovative page designs. A key autobiographic comic of the Francophone tradition.

Exit Wounds (2007). Writer and Illustrator: Rutu Modan. Drawn and Quarterly

Rutu Modan tells an unlikely love story in present-day Israel in a delicate, rather reduced ligne-claire style, which makes surprising use of gutters and mise-en-page.

Fables (2002–). Writer: Bill Willingham. Illustrator: Mark Buckingham et al. DC Vertigo

In *Fables*, the fairy-tale characters have grown up and moved into contemporary New York. Prince Charming has been divorced three times, Snow White has married the Big Bad Wolf, and Cinderella has become a glamorous secret agent. Drawing on popular genres like heroic fantasy, spy thrillers, and romantic comedy, *Fables* brings the fairy tale characters and their stories into the contemporary world.

Fun Home: A Family Tragicomic (2007). Writer and Illustrator: Alison Bechdel. Houghton Mifflin

Alison Bechdel chronicles her coming to terms with her father's death and her own sexuality as a lesbian in this autobiographical comic. Bechdel's long-running series, *Dykes to Watch Out For* (1983–2008), addresses lesbian and feminist issues, and is similarly sharply observed and shrewdly commented as *Fun Home*.

Gemma Bovary (1999). Writer and Illustrator: Posy Simmonds. Jonathan Cape

Gemma Bovary is an adaptation of Gustave Flaubert's novel *Madame Bovary* which revolves around the adultery, mounting debt, and melodramatic suicide of Emma Bovary. In her adaptation, Simmonds retells the story with an Englishwoman in France in the role of Emma, and she uses the perspective of Raymond, who knows Flaubert's novel well and intervenes in Gemma's life, in order to interpret the events. The comic was first serialized in the British newspaper the *Guardian*.

Ghost World (1997). Writer and Illustrator: Daniel Clowes. Fantagraphics

Ghost World presents the teenage angst and cynicism of Enid Coleslaw and Rebecca Doppelmeyer, and their experience of growing up in the contemporary US. The comic was previously serialized in Clowes' comic book *Eightball* (1993–7).

Jimmy Corrigan, the Smartest Kid on Earth (2000). Writer and Illustrator: Chris Ware. Pantheon Books

Chris Ware's distinct, strongly reduced drawing style and his use of panel sequence for detaining, rather than dramatizing, action comes to the fore in this graphic novel on the life of Jimmy Corrigan, and his family, who is always waiting for something exciting to happen but inevitably disappointed. The comic was serialized in Chris Ware's self-published comic book *Acme Novelty Library* (1995–2000), before it was published in a trade paperback.

Kabuki (1994–) Writer and Illustrator: David Mack. Image Comics

Kabuki is a Western engagement with the culture of Japan in comics. Rather than relying on the visual style of manga, it sets its story in a world where Japanese mythology, technology, and the crime syndicates of the Yakuza meet. *Kabuki*'s drawing style and mise-en-page are innovative, and often make use of highly symbolic elements.

The League of Extraordinary Gentlemen (1999–). Writer: Alan Moore. Illustrator: Kevin O'Neill. ABC Comics/DC/Wildstorm (1999–2007); Top Shelf (2007–)

The League of Extraordinary Gentlemen series chronicles the adventures of a secret organization of fictional characters and their crusade against villainy in British history. In the first volume, for example, Mina Harker (from *Dracula*), Alan Quartermain (from *King Solomon's Mines*), Dr. Jekyll and Mr. Hyde, Captain Nemo and others team up to keep Victorian London safe. *The Black Dossier* chronicles the history of the "league" back to the Elizabethan Age, while the first, second, and third volume extends from the mid-nineteenth century to the entire twentieth century.

The Life and Opinions of Tristram Shandy, Gentleman (1997) Writer and Illustrator: Martin Rowson. SelfMadeHero

Rowson's adaptation of Laurence Sterne's novel brings both the self-reflexivity and the discursiveness of Sterne's narrator into the comics form. He also draws on eighteenth-century visual culture, from battle paintings to Hogarth's engravings, as well as contemporary cultures of academic criticism and film-making, in order to comment on and situate his story. Rowson has also adapted Swift's *Gulliver's Travels* and T.S. Eliot's *The Wasteland*.

Little Nemo in Slumberland (1905–14). Writer and Illustrator: Winsor McCay. Large-format edition: *Little Nemo in Slumberland: So Many Splendid Sundays* (Sunday Press Books, 2005). Various other editions from Fantagraphics.

Winsor McCay's most famous work, *Little Nemo in Slumberland* tells of the travels of a little boy in his dreamlands. He encounters strange creatures, embarks on a quest for a princess, and lives through fantastic adventures. At the end of every installment, Little Nemo wakes up and finds himself in his bed, safe from the strange threats of Slumberland but also bereft of its magic.

Love and Rockets (1982–). Writers and Illustrators: Gilbert and Jaime Hernandez. Fantagraphics.

Love and Rockets presents the Latino culture in the United States in the comics format. The stories in the series center around Latino communities, focusing on different individual experiences. One of the first, and most important alternative comics series, *Love and Rockets* has been running intermittently since 1982.

Masterpiece Comics (2009). Writer and Illustrator: R.I. Sikoryak. Drawn and Quarterly.

First published as individual comics in various comics magazines, such as Art Spiegelman and Françoise Mouly's *RAW*, R.I. Sikoryak's *Masterpiece Comics* presents famous pieces of world literature in the distinct styles of famous comics: Dostoyevky's *Crime and Punishment* is presented as a Batman comic, Frank Kafka's *The Metamorphosis* in the style of *Peanuts*, or Camus's philosophical works on a series of *Superman* covers.

Maus: A Survivor's Tale (1986 and 1991). Writer and Illustrator: Art Spiegelman. Pantheon Books

Art Spiegelman's autobiographic comic of his father's account of the Holocaust was first serialized in Spiegelman and Mouly's comic magazine *RAW*, and then published in two volumes (1986: *My Father Bleeds History* and 1991: *And Here*

My Troubles Began). Current editions combine both volumes into a single book. The comic won the Pulitzer Prize Special Award in 1992.

Palestine (1992). Writer and Illustrator: Joe Sacco. Fantagraphics

Joe Sacco is a comics artist famous for his journalistic work, both on the Palestine conflict (with *Palestine* and *Footnotes on Gaza*) and the Bosnian war (with *Safe Area Goražde*). His expressionist style creates a fruitful tension with the documentary impetus of journalism and opens a striking perspective on what it means to experience these events.

Persepolis (2000) Writer and Illustrator: Marjane Satrapi. L'Association / Pantheon

Marjane Satrapi tells about her experience of growing up in Iran as the daughter of Westernized parents after the Islamization of the country, as well as her emigration to Europe. The English-language version has been published in two volumes: *Persepolis 1* and *Persepolis 2*. Satrapi's style features strong black/white contrasts, and her storyworld is both funny and fantastic. A film adaptation of both volumes of *Persepolis* has been released in 2007, with Satrapi herself as the co-director.

Planetary (1998–2009). Writer: Warren Ellis. Illustrator: John Cassaday. Wildstorm / DC

The Planetary team is a group of superheroes who tag themselves as "Archeologists of the Impossible." They unearth the fictional history of the twentieth century, including Hong Kong films, pulp adventure novels and the superhero genre itself, and explore the alternative storyworlds of the multiverse.

Prince Valiant (1937–). Writer and Illustrator: Hal Forster. Fantagraphics (collected edition in five volumes)

Set in the mythical past of the Arthurian legend, *Prince Valiant* chronicles the adventures of a young man on his way to Camelot and his later exploits as a knight. A rich sense of detail and splendid vistas of castles and crowds pervade Forster's drawings. From the 1970s onwards, other artists continued the series.

Promethea (1999–2005). Writer: Alan Moore. Illustrators: J.H. Williams III and Mike Gray. ABC Comics/Wildstorm/DC

In *Promethea*, the heroine explores the history of comics and the wonders of the human imagination. A gorgeously drawn and colored comic, in which

Alan Moore tackles the big questions of life, its meaning, and what comes after it. *Promethea* is one of the series which Moore started for his ABC (America's Best Comics) project. ABC recreates an entire comics universe, featuring series like *The League of Extraordinary Gentlemen*, *Tom Strong*, and *Top 10*.

Pyongyang (2003). Writer and Illustrator: Guy Delisle. Jonathan Cape

Guy Delisle's account of his stay in North Korea (as supervisor in an animation company) reflects on his experience as a foreigner and the perspective he gains on everyday life in a totalitarian society. In his autobiographical comic, Delisle highlights the absurdities and dark ironies of everyday life in the communist state. Comparisons to George Orwell's *1984* come to mind with Delisle's matter-of-fact style.

The Rabbi's Cat (2003). Writer and Illustrator: Joann Sfar. Pantheon Books

Set in Algiers in the 1930s, this charming story features a rabbi, his cat, and his daughter. Its prolific author Joann Sfar has also adapted Saint-Exupéry's *The Little Prince* and Voltaire's *Candide* into comics.

Rodolphe Töpffer: The Complete Comic Strips (2007). Writer and Illustrator: Rodolphe Töpffer. Edited by David Kunzle. Jackson: University of Mississippi Press

This volume collects the comics of the nineteenth-century Swiss author Rodolphe Töpffer, who is hailed by scholars like Thierry Groensteen as the inventor of comics.

The Sandman (1989–96). Writer: Neil Gaiman. Illustrators: Dave McKean, Marc Dringenberg et al. DC Vertigo

The Sandman relaunched an earlier superhero series of the same name, but it reimagined the superhero as Dream of the Endless, a mythical personification of the human capacity to dream. The series chronicles Dream's last years, as he breaks free from imprisonment, strives to regain his power and finally falls prey to his own mistakes. Its tragic narrative ties into history, mythology, and world literature and explores the cultural importance of storytelling as such.

Sense and Sensibility (2010). Writer: Nancy Butler. Illustrator: Sonny Liew. Marvel Comics

The Marvel adaptation of Jane Austen's novel has been scripted by contemporary romance author Nancy Butler. Other adaptations include *Pride and Prejudice* (2009), *Emma* (2011), and *Northanger Abbey* (2011–12).

Siberia (2004). Writer and Illustrator: Nikolai Maslov. Soft Skull Press

An autobiographical narrative of Maslov's youth in Russia, which features a striking drawing style in grey pencil wash.

Sinfest (2000–). Writer and Illustrator: Tatsuya Ishida. Web. Dark Horse Comics (*Sinfest* Volume 1 and Volume 2; *Viva La Resistance*)

Sinfest is a long-running web comic, telling humorous stories about a set of characters which includes the Devil and Jesus. It is published on a daily rota, with one comic strip every weekday and a colored full page on Sunday.

The Spirit (1940–52). Writer and Illustrator: Will Eisner. DC Comics

The Spirit is a vigilante figure in the tradition of the pulp magazines and the hard-boiled novel. He encounters disturbing villains and exciting women in his nightly adventures across New York. *The Spirit* started as a newspaper supplement, running from 1940. It displays Will Eisner's skill as a draughtsman and composer of title images, as well as his sense of humor.

Superman: Red Son (2003). Writer: Mark Millar. Illustrators: Dave Johnson, Kilian Plunkett et al. DC Comics

This alternative worlds story answers the question "what if Superman had landed on earth not in the US, but in the USSR?" Mark Millar spins a counterfactual tale about Superman's youth in the Ukraine, his rise to power as Stalin's right-hand man and his encounter with a Batman-dissident, and thereby uncovers the totalitarian tendencies in Superman himself.

Terry and the Pirates (1934–46). Writer and Illustrator: Milton Caniff. IDW Publishing

Perhaps Milton Caniff's most famous series, *Terry and the Pirates* presents the adventures of young Terry in the exotic, far-away lands of Eastern Asia, in particular China. Later works of Caniff, such as *Steve Canyon*, would take up similar themes of exploration and adventure.

Transmetropolitan (1997–2002). Writer: Warren Ellis. Illustrator: Darick Robertson. Vertigo: DC Comics

In *Transmetropolitan*, Warren Ellis presents a bad-future rendition of today's media world. Spider Jerusalem, a jaded star reporter who is disgusted by society, emerges from his retreat in the forest, and takes up the fight with the political establishment and good taste.

V for Vendetta (1982–9). Writer: Alan Moore. Illustrator: David Lloyd. DC Comics

V for Vendetta is set in a Britain of the future, where the fascist party has taken over power and established a totalitarian state. It tells the story of Evey, an orphan struggling to survive in this dystopian world, and V, a man out for revenge and plotting to bring down the system. *V for Vendetta* addresses issues such as the importance of beauty and the arts as a countermodel to the pragmatic, politicized environment of the totalitarian state.

Watchmen (1986). Writer: Alan Moore. Illustrator: Dave Gibbons. Colors: John Higgins. DC Comics. An *Absolute Watchmen* edition came out in 2005

Watchmen tells the story of a group of superheroes investigating the murder of one of their members. Set at the time of the Cold War, the superheroes negotiate their different understandings of what it means to be a hero and they have to come to terms with a society which does not want them anymore. This is one of the most important texts of the superhero genre.

Glossary

*Asterisked words cross-reference other entries of this glossary.

180-DEGREE RULE. The rule has been developed for film but can also be applied to panel sequences in comics. It entails that dialogues are supposed to be shown from one side of an imaginary line between both characters only. Shots from different positions along this line describing the 180-degree angle (such as alternating overshoulder shots) can be edited together, in order to render the exchange more dynamic, but if the camera crosses the line, this is usually perceived as disruptive by viewers.

ADAPTATION. When a *NARRATIVE is transported from one *MEDIUM into another, this is called adaptation. Because different media have different *AFFORDANCES, an adaptation always has to make changes to the original text, be it in condensing or extending the events or in changing the style of narration.

AFFORDANCE. A media affordance refers to the specific features and properties of a *MEDIUM, or *MODE, and the capabilities for storytelling they entail. Rendering a story in images or words means that some features of *NARRATIVE will be easier to achieve and some will be more difficult. The possibilities and limitations of media and modes are crucial for *ADAPTATIONS. See *MODE.

ALTERNATIVE COMICS. Comics which posit themselves as an alternative to the *MAINSTREAM, either as being more unconventional in style, or as more controversial in subject matter. Like *INDEPENDENT COMICS, they would usually be creator-owned and not written on commission.

Studying Comics and Graphic Novels, First Edition. Karin Kukkonen.
© 2013 John Wiley & Sons, Ltd. Published 2013 by John Wiley & Sons, Ltd.

ANCHORAGE. In Roland Barthes's terminology, anchorage occurs between the *MODES of images and words when one mode specifies the other, when it "anchors" its meaning. See also *RELAY.

AUTOBIOGRAPHICAL PACT. The tacit agreement between the author of an autobiography and her readers that the author, the first person *NARRATOR and the main *CHARACTER of the autobiography are all the same person, and that he or she is going to recount the events truthfully.

AUTOGRAPHY. A term for self-drawn autobiographical comics. Not only do these comics tell a story about the authors themselves, but they are also created in every aspect (words, images, lettering, etc.) as a personal expression of the authors.

BANDE DESSINÉE. The French word for comics. In English, it is used to refer to French-language comics.

BODY SCHEMA. Our pre-conscious knowledge of how our body is positioned in space and in relation to other objects. When we navigate the physical (and cultural) world around us, we make use of our body schema, as realized in our motorsensory capacities, but we are usually not aware of it.

BRITISH INVASION. In the context of comics, this term refers to the importance of British comics writers on US mainstream comics from the 1980s onwards, such as Alan Moore, Neil Gaiman, or Warren Ellis.

CAPTION. A little box of written text, often located in the top-left corner of a *PANEL. Other than the text in *SPEECH BUBBLES, the text in the captions is not located in the time and space represented in the panel image. However, it often refers to and comments on the event presented in the panel.

CHARACTERS. Characters are storyworld participants. They set the events of the story in motion in their interactions, and relate to these events through their intentions and emotional responses. Characters are often understood to have a particular set of psychological features, which give them something like an identity, and in the story, they are often placed into moral hierarchies (good-evil) in relation to one another.

CLUES. In the terminology used in this book, clues refer to the elements on the comics page which readers pick up and draw *INFERENCES from in the meaning-making process. Any element on the comics page can work as a clue, suggesting inferences and becoming salient for reader.

COGNITIVE COMPLEXITY. The different layers of intentions and mental states that come together when *CHARACTERS interact, and try to second-guess or simply understand each other, create cognitive complexity, or as Lisa Zunshine calls it "socio-cognitive complexity." Readers try to track who knows what about whom in order to get a sense of the social relations, mental states, and intentionalities of an encounter. *NARRATORS, who want to communicate something about these encounters as well, add another layer to cognitive complexity.

COMIC BOOK. A publication format of the comics *MEDIUM, which resembles the magazine and in which a limited number of pages is used to present (part of) a *NARRATIVE. Often, the narrative is serialized and its installments are often later collected into so-called "trade paperbacks."

COMICS. A *MEDIUM narrating its stories through images, words, and sequence. As a medium, comics have a particular combination of media *MODES, a particular set of technologies devoted to their creation and distribution, and a particular set of institutions, such as publishing houses and sales venues, which have developed around them. Formats of the comics medium are *COMIC STRIPS, *COMIC BOOKS, the *GRAPHIC NOVEL, and *WEB COMICS.

COMICS CODE. A set of rules, concerning depictions of violence and sex, to which comics publishers have complied in self-censorship since 1954. The Code has been updated since and, in recent years, frequently ignored.

COMICS CREATORS. Creating a comic requires many steps, from outlining the *NARRATIVE to designing the page-layout, drawing the panel images, inking their outlines, coloring them, and lettering the *SPEECH BUBBLES. In some cases, such as *ALTERNATIVE COMICS, a single creator performs all these roles. In other cases, such as *MAINSTREAM COMICS, the creative process is often partitioned out between different creators with an editor for the series overseeing the production of the comic.

COMIC STRIP. A single row of comics *PANELS belonging together in a (narrative) sequence. Comic strips are the most common format for newspaper comics.

COMPOSITION. The particular relation of individual visual elements to each other, depending on their position on the page or in the panel image. These relations form meaningful compositions, suggesting power relationships between characters, lines of movement, or points of interest in an image.

CONCEPTUAL METAPHOR. See *METAPHOR.

CONTINUITY EDITING. A style of film editing that creates a flow between different shots and prevents disruptive effects in combining different angles and shot sizes. *POINT OF VIEW-EDITING and the *180- DEGREE RULE belong to the set of techniques known as continuity editing. It has been developed for film in early Hollywood cinema, but also comics have taken up some of its conventions.

CURIOSITY. In the narratological sense, curiosity is readers' attention to a gap in the past of the narrative. It cues readers to establish causal *INFERENCES which will fill the gap and account for the chain of events leading to the narrative present. See *PLOT.

DEICTIC GAZE. When a *character is looking at something, a process of joint attention leads readers follow the gaze of that character in order to see what she is looking at. In comics, the deictic gaze can either work within the setting of an individual *PANEL to highlight important features in the image, but the deictic gaze can also work across panels, guiding readers to pay attention to connections on the page which the character herself (in the panel) could not have possibly seen.

DEFAMILIARIZATION. Rendering the conventions of narrative or artistic techniques visible to the reader is called "defamiliarization." In this process, something that is so familiar to readers that they don't even notice it anymore suddenly becomes strange and noteworthy. Formalism has established defamiliarization as a hallmark of the literariness of language.

DÉNOUEMENT. A term for the resolution of the *PLOT. Literally, dénoument means "disentanglement," and it refers to the strands of plot being unraveled at the end of a *NARRATIVE.

DISCOURSE. The surface structure of a *NARRATIVE with all the details and specificities of the *NARRATOR's telling of the events. This is the narrative as it presents itself to readers. If the *STORY is the *what* of a narrative (what is told?), then the discourse is the *how* of narrative (how is it presented?). Some narratologists posit the *PLOT as the level between story and discourse on which the events of the story are restructured, but which is not yet the narrator's detailed discourse.

EMBODIMENT. Embodiment refers to the ways in which the images and words of a comics narrative affects and engages with the readers' own bodily experience. See *MIRROR NEURONS; *BODY SCHEMA.

FIDELITY. Considering an *ADAPTATION in terms of fidelity means asking the question of how "true" to the original from a different *MEDIUM the comics version is. Posing the fidelity question often already gives the original text precedence over the adaptation. An alternative take on adaptation is to understand it as a "translation," not a reproduction, of the original.

FLASHBACK / FLASHFORWARD. A flashback occurs when the *NARRATIVE jumps backwards in time, for example, when a *CHARACTER retells his experience of events in the past. A flashforward occurs, when the narrative presents events which lie in the future of the main storyline. Flashforward and flashback mark a disjuncture of *STORY and *DISCOURSE: the *NARRATOR'S discourse does not follow the order of the story, but jumps back or forward. Gérard Genette calls this phenomenon "analepsis."

FOCALIZER. The projected instance who experiences the events and within whose limits of experiences the *NARRATIVE is recounted. The perspective the focalizer gives on the events and its limitation of knowledge is called "focalization." A focalizer can, but doesn't have to, be the same instance as the *NARRATOR. Sometimes, first-person narrators know more than the *CHARACTER could know; sometimes, third-person narrators present a stretch of narrative through the experience of a particular character. In these cases, narration and focalization are distinct. See *NARRATOR; see *OBSERVER.

FRANKFURT SCHOOL. A group of cultural critics, most prominently Max Horkheimer, Theodor Adorno and Jurgen Habermas, who understand popular mass culture as a potential threat against political awareness.

GENRE. A kind of narrative, which implies particular character types, particular conflicts, and standard situations, as well as particular probabilities of actions and particular ways in which the "reality" of a *STORYWORLD can be represented. Superhero comics are an example for a dominant genre in the comics *MEDIUM. As soon as readers identify a *NARRATIVE as belonging to a particular genre, the patterns of this genre will influence the kinds of *INFERENCES they draw.

GESTALT. A constellation of elements which forms a coherent whole in perception. Human perception chunks visual elements together into groups, looking for patterns and connections. It is possible to arrive at multiple gestalts for a single constellation of elements, but it seems we cannot process two different gestalts at the same time. Gestalt psychology at the beginning of the twentieth century has investigated these phenomena of perception.

GRAPHIATION. The distinct individual style of a comics author (or *NARRATOR) which marks a comics *NARRATIVE as his or her utterance. Graphiation extends to the use of colors, and the kinds of lines and contours chosen, and it has been conceived in analogy to "enunciation" in language.

GRAPHIC NOVEL. A publication format of the comics *MEDIUM, which is a self-contained, non-serialized comics *NARRATIVE. Commonly, however, it is used to refer to any page-based comic.

GUTTER. The space between the *PANELS. Sometimes, when panels are clearly demarked by panel frames, the gutter is rendered as a white space between the panels. Sometimes, panels are layered on top of each other or not clearly demarked, and then it is more difficult to discern the gutter.

HETEROGLOSSIA. Mikhail Bakhtin's term for bringing together multiple speech-styles and perspectives in a narrative. Unlike a single, monopolizing perspective imposing meaning, the multiple perspectives in heteroglossia interact, throwing different, contrasting lights on the events. Other related terms in Bakhtin's theories are "dialogism" and "polyphony." Bakhtin considers heteroglossia to be a particular feature of the novel.

HOMODIEGETIC / HETERODIEGETIC. This distinction, introduced by Genette, refers to whether the *NARRATOR is located inside the *STORYWORLD or outside of it. Genette calls the storyworld "diegesis," and therefore narrators that are part of the storyworld as characters are "homodiegetic" and narrators that are not part of the storyworld are "heterodiegetic" (from the Greek "homo" – same and "hetero" – different). See *STORYWORLD; see *NARRATOR.

INDEPENDENT COMICS. Comics which are published by a non-*MAINSTREAM publishing house. Often, the tag "independent comics" also implies that these comics are creator-owned and not written on commission, as are for example the superhero comics.

INFERENCES. The conclusions readers draw on the basis of the *CLUES of the comics page. In the process of making sense of what we see on the page and of projecting the further development of the scenario, inferences are the threads that tie the comic's *NARRATIVE together. Inferences in comics narrative are drawn within the framework of the *STORYWORLD.

MAINSTREAM COMICS. Comics which are published by the biggest publishing houses, mostly DC and Marvel, and which would be read by a significant proportion of the overall population of comics readers. Other than

*INDEPENDENT, *ALTERNATIVE, or *UNDERGROUND COMICS, describing a comic as "mainstream" implies that it is a conventional, uncontroversial work (which is not necessarily the case).

MANGA. The term for "Japanese comics," meaning either comics originally created in Japan or comics created in the style typical for Japanese comics.

MEDIUM. A *MODE of communication with a particular set of technologies and institutions connected to their creation, distribution and consumption. Examples of media are book, film, TV, and *COMICS.

METALEPSIS. When the boundary of the *STORYWORLD is crossed, metalepsis occurs. This crossing of boundaries can occur from the storyworld into the world of the telling, for example when a *CHARACTER addresses authors or readers, or from the world of the telling into the storyworld, for example when an author enters the storyworld and (ostentatiously) intervenes in the events.

METANARRATION. When a *NARRATOR refers to the fact that he or she is narrating, this is called "metanarration." Attention is then called to any of the functions of the narrator: the way they create the *STORYWORLD, the fact that they communicate them to readers, and problem that they need to vouch for their narrative's authenticity.

METAPHOR. A stylistic device which allows you to see something in terms of something else, comparing the two. In cognitive metaphor theory, metaphors are understood as two conceptual domains being compared, for example "Anger" and "Hot Liquid in a Container". The connection between the two domains forms a conceptual metaphor, and features from one domain are mapped onto the other. Anger, for example, is understood in terms of heat and pressure here. Conceptual metaphors are then rendered in so-called metaphorical expressions, which can be either verbal ("boiling with anger") or visual (a character with steam coming out of his ears).

MIRROR NEURONS. Neurons which fire in our brain when we observe an action, similar to the act of performing it. Mirror neurons are one explanation for the embodied echo of actions we perceive, and this suggests that – to some extent – readers experience what they see on the comics page. The scientific evidence for mirror neurons is still debated and its remains to be seen how far-reaching the aesthetic and cultural conclusions are which can legitimately be drawn from the existence of mirror neurons.

MISE EN PAGE. The French term for the page layout in *COMICS. It concerns the particular ways in which *PANELS are placed on the surface of the page, either next to each other or superimposed on each other. Mise en page is meaningful in comics, because the relation of panels suggests different *INFERENCES.

MODE. A mode is a set of semiotic resources, such as images or words, selected in order to tell a story. Most *MEDIA make use of more than one mode. Comics are a multi-modal medium, because they employ images, words, and sequence. Different modes (and media) have different *AFFORDANCES.

MULTIVERSE. A set of alternative *STORYWORLDS, in which alternative versions of (superhero) *CHARACTERS and their stories are located.

NARRATIVE. A chain of events that involves a complication or a conflict and that is told by a *NARRATOR. A narrative develops a *PLOT, a causality of events, presents *CHARACTERS and their intentions and is located in a *STORYWORLD. Narrative is often understood as a particular process for making meaning of our personal experiences, of our cultural worlds and of our historical past.

NARRATOR. The (more or less) personalized projection of the teller of the story. Narrators are distinct from *FOCALIZERS and *OBSERVERS, even though sometimes the same *CHARACTER or instance can take up all these functions. Narrators are categorized as being located inside the *STORYWORLD (homodiegetic) and outside the storyworld (heterodiegetic), and as personalized and depersonalized. Their functions are to create the *NARRATIVE, to communicate it, and to vouch for the authenticity of the narrative they tell.

OBSERVER. The projected instance whose point of view is cued in a panel image. Usually, panel images do not mark the point of view from which they are perceived but we consider this element of visual information to be neutral. When the observer position is marked, usually only for a single panel, readers are given a very particular vantage point on the *STORYWORLD.

ONOMATOPOETIC EFFECT. Onomatopoeia is a word or phrase whose sound reflects its meaning, such as "quacking." Comics sometimes feature onomatopoeia such as "wham!" or "argh." The size and shape of these letters underlines the specific qualities of these sounds.

PANEL. The basic unit of the comics page, panels are the boxes in which images and words in comics are located. Sometimes, they are enclosed by a panel frame; sometimes, they are not. Putting together several panels, either in rows or more freely across the page, leads to sequence, a basic feature of comics storytelling.

Personalized / Depersonalized narrator. Narrators who are fully fleshed out as *characters, and who talk of their experience in the first person, are personalized narrators. Narrators who take back their personal voice and project an outside view on the *storyworld in the third person, are depersonalized narrators.

Plot. The strings of events that are entangled and complicated, and then resolved, in the course of a *narrative. In terms of narrative theory, plot falls between *story (the skeleton of the events) and *discourse (its surface presentation), arranging them in an interesting and meaningful pattern which is capable of eliciting *suspense (How is it going to continue or end?), *curiosity (What has happened?) and *surprise (Did this happen?).

Point-of-view editing. This technique of combining camera shots creates the impression that a *character (seen in one shot) is looking at something or someone (seen in the other shot), and illustrates who knows what in a *storyworld. In full POV-editing, we see the shot of a character looking, then the shot of what she is looking at, and then perhaps another shot of the character responding to what she has seen. Sometimes, there are only the first two shots, for example, when a character is looking for something and finds it; sometimes, there are only the last two shots, for example, when what we see on the screen is revealed to be the observation of a particular character.

Popular culture. A term referring to widely spread and widely received cultural artifacts, such as *comics, and the cultural practices surrounding them. Often, popular culture is understood as the opposite of high culture and takes the bottom place in hierarchies of cultural value.

Pregnant moment. English translation of Lessing's "fruchtbarer Augenblick." In order to be suggestive, an image has to present a "pregnant moment," which allows readers to project the further course of events from the moment of the action which is captured in the image.

Proto-comics. Cultural artifacts, such as the Bayeux tapestry or Trajan's column, which display features of comics storytelling, but which are not *comics themselves because they do not use the technologies of and are not part of the institutions around comics.

Relay. In Roland Barthes's terminology, instances when two *modes like images and words interact in meaning-making on an even footing. See also *anchorage.

Sans paroles From the French, meaning "without words." Sans paroles are
*comics which work only through images in sequence, but do not employ
the written word. Sometimes, regular comics have passages which feature no
*speech bubbles or *captions in order to achieve effects such as the
slowing down or speeding up of action, of rendering stillness or a poetic,
delicate quality of the situation.

Speech bubble. The area in a panel image in which the written dialogue of the
*characters is represented. The written text is in the "body" of the speech
bubble; its "tail" connects to the speaker of the utterance. Other than the text
in *captions, the text in speech bubbles is located in the time and space of
the panel image. The text in speech bubbles is sometimes lettered in a
particular way to convey volume of speech (*onomatopoetic effects), emotional states or the quality of the sound.

Speed line. Lines connecting, and thereby indicating, various consecutive
positions a *character takes in a single panel. They can suggest movement,
speed, and force.

Story. The story is the skeleton of events which underlies a *narrative. As we
read the surface, the detailed *discourse of a narrative, we reconstruct the
story. If the discourse is the *how* of a narrative (How is it presented?), then
the story is the *what* of a narrative (What is told?).

Storyworld. The fictional world in which the events of a *narrative take
place. When reading, we develop a mental model, within which we draw our
*inferences, and this is the storyworld. The storyworld is distinct from the
real world; we immerse ourselves in it when reading, and several storyworlds
can be embedded within each other, when stories within a story are told. See
*metalepsis.

Superheroes. A genre in the comics *medium which features *characters
with extraordinary powers, and whose adventures revolve around the
protection of a community from evil forces. Superheroes are highly politicized because these comics often address issues of power and ideology.

Surprise. Surprise occurs when a gap in *plot development is suddenly made
salient, i.e., when readers are confronted with something unexpected.
See plot.

Suspense. Suspense works as an uncertainty in *plot development, i.e., when
the readers are kept guessing as to how the narrative will continue. See plot.

THOUGHT BUBBLE. Similar to a *SPEECH BUBBLE, the written text in a thought bubble is located in the time and space of the panel image. The words, however, form the thoughts of a *CHARACTER and are not communicated to the other characters. In the thought bubble, the tail of the speech bubble becomes a series of dots and its body is often rendered in the shape of a cloud.

UNDERGROUND COMICS. Comics which emerged from within the underground movement of the 1960s, also called "comix." These comics direct themselves not only against *MAINSTREAM COMICS but also against mainstream morality. *ALTERNATIVE COMICS have, partially, developed out of this tradition.

WEB COMICS. Comics which are distributed in digital form through the world-wide web. Sometimes, they are also created entirely in digital form and make use of its particular *AFFORDANCES (such as hypertext, scrolling the screen, or animations).

Index

The numbers in bold indicate the pages on which the entry in question is defined.

adaptation, 3, **73**, 80, 83–84, 86, 94
  as translation 81
  fidelity in 80, 81, 83–84, 94
affordance, *see* media affordances
Ally Sloper, 74, 103–104, 124
alternative comics, 4, **56–57**, 68
Arnold, Matthew, 115–117, 153
authencity (of narration), 3, 42, 44, 55,
    67, 69
author, 6, **32**, 39, 55, 60, 65, 68
autobiographical comics, 2–3, 6, 39,
    55–57, 60, 65, 68–70, 118
autobiographical pact, 57, 65
autobiography, 56, 57
autographic agent, 59–60
autography, **56**

Bad Machinery, 11, 12, 15
background, 18–19, 66
Bakhtin, Mikhail, 24
Barsalou, Lawrence, 152–153
Barthes, Roland, 34
Bayeux tapestry, 99–100
Blankets, 3, 55, 60–61, 62–64, 68, 69
body schema, 8, 24, 60, 130, 151–153

Bourdieu, Pierre, 133–134
Bordwell, David, 35, 44
Brinkley, Nell, 103
British Invasion, 118–119
Brooks, Cleanth, 150–151, 153
Busch, Wilhelm, 102

caption, 8, 24, 34, 39
cartoons, 102, 104
character, 22, 24–25, 36, 74
character,
    fictional mind of, 16, 25, 55, 130
    gazes of, **13**, 15–16, 18, 79
    relation between 8–10, 16, 23–24,
      47, 61, 79
Classics Illustrated, 83–84, 114–115
close reading, 2, 7, 126, 150
closure, **10–11**, 47
clues, 7–8, 29, 31, 32, 149, 152, 154
cognitive approach to comics, 1–2, 7–9
cognitive complexity, 73, 85–86, 88,
    90, 94
comic analysis, 2, 7–8, 23, 149–150, 154
comic book 38, 74–75, 80, 84–85, 100,
    106–107, 111, 124

Studying Comics and Graphic Novels, First Edition. Karin Kukkonen.
© 2013 John Wiley & Sons, Ltd. Published 2013 by John Wiley & Sons, Ltd.

comics,
  as literature, 85, 90, 94, 149, 153–154
  as medium, 4–5, 73, 75, 94, 99, 102
  as popular culture, 3, 83, 84, 99,
    102, 104, 112, 113–115, 119,
    133–134, 149
  as visual language, 4–5
  censorship of, 110–111, 114
  critical approaches to, 125–127
  definition of, 4–5, 102
  history of, 3, 99–119, 131–132
  medium specific elements of, 24–25,
    100–101
  re–evaluation of, 57, 69–70, 85,
    99, 150
comics code, 111, 113–114, 117,
  118–119
comics creators, 5–6, 39; see also: author
composition, **9**, 11–12, 19, 34,
  79–80, 152
conceptual metaphor *see* metaphor
continuity, 109
continuity editing, 47, 59
convergence culture, 73–74, 149
Crumb, Robert, 56, 117
curiosity, 35–36

defamiliarization, 73, **93**, 94
Desolation Jones, 16, 17, 18, 29, 30
discourse *see* story and discourse

EC Comics, 43, 44, 46, 81–83, 107,
  111–114, 119
Eisner, Will, 55, 84–85
Eliot, T.S., 153
embodiment, **9**, 25, 29–30, 59, 60–61,
  69, 91, 93, 130, 150–152
emotions, 15–16, 25, 129, 150, 152–153

facial expressions, 9, **15–16**, 19, 88
facial features, 15
fact-fiction distinction, 48, 66–67, 69

flashback, 35
flashforward, 35
focalization, **45**, 57, 59–60, 79–80,
  128–129
focalizer, **45**, 57, 59
Forceville, Charles, 129
foreground *see* background
Forster, E.M., 48
Frankenstein, 114–115
Frankfurt School, 116–117
Freud, Sigmund, 134, 136
Fun Home, 3, 55, 57, 58, 61, 66, 68, 69

Gaines, William, 107, 111–113
gaze *see* character, gaze of
Genette, Gérard, 35, 39, 45
gestalt psychology, 10–11, 18–19
gestures, 9, 61
graphiation, 56
graphic novel, 4, 84–85, 124
Greimas, Algirdas, 37
Groensteen, Thierry, 126
gutter, **10**, 18, 151

Heilman, Robert, 150–151, 153
Herman, David, 12, 129
heteroglossia, 24
high culture *see* popular culture and
  high culture
Hogarth, William, 102
horror comics *see* EC Comics

image angle, 46, 60–61
image size, 3, 9, 39, 46
independent comics, 57
inferences, 7–8, 10, 12, 15, 18, 19,
  22–24, 29, 129, 149–150
irony, 23, 24, 86, 88, 90

Kirby, Jack, 55

Jenkins, Henry, 73

Labov, William, 37, 48
Lacan, Jacques, 136
Laocoön, 13–14
Lessing, Gotthard Ephraim, 14
lettering, 9, 55
Little Nemo in Slumberland, 6, 104,
    105, 126, 128, 130–133, 134, 135,
    136, 138
Lubbock, Percy, 31–32, 49

mainstream comics, 4–5, 56–57,
    118–119
manga, 6, 55
Marston, William, 150, 153
Maus, 3, 55, 56–57, 65–69, 85,
    123–124, 134
McCay, Winsor, 6, 103–104, 124,
    131–132
McCloud, Scott, 10
media affordances, 3, 4, 14, **73**, 74, **75**,
    80, 90, 94, 128
medium, 4–5, 75
mental model, **11–12**, 19
Menu, Jean-Christophe, 69–70
metalepsis, 65
metanarration, **42**
metaphor, **23**, 25, 96–97, 101, 112,
    129, 134
mise en page, **19**, 61, 80, 88, 93, 103,
    126, 128, 132, 151–152
modes (media), 75, 88, 106
multiverse, 109

narration, **44**, 45, 79–80
narrative, 2, 10, **12**, 31, 32, 36, 38,
    73, 129
  as meaning-making, 48–49, 66–67
narrative context, 16
narrative probabilities, 22, 32, 36
narratology, 32, **35–36**, 128–129
narrator, 31, 32, 39, 42, 45, 59–60, 61,
    69, 88, 90, 93, 128

depersonalized, **44**
functions of, 32, 69
heterodiegetic, **39**, 42, 44, 79
homodiegetic, **39**, 42, 44, 46, 79
personalized, **42**, 44, 82, 93
rhetoric of, 32, 44, 49, 55, 69
newspaper comics, 103–104, 106, 115,
    119, 124, 132

observer, **45**, 47, 49, 59–60
180-degree rule, 47–48

page, as narrative unit, 23, 80, 90, 94
page layout *see* mise en page
perspective, 13, 39, 42, 45, 57, 59, 66
plot, 31, 34–36, 38, 66, 80, 93
point of view, **45**, 57, 59, 129
point-of-view editing, 45, **47**
pop-art, 117
popular culture, 114, 116–117
  and high culture, 83, 84, 85,
    114–117, 119, 134
pregnant moment, 14–15, 47, 74, 79–80
Prince, Gerald, 12, 35
Promethea, 140–141, 143, 150, 152–153
Propp, Vladimir, 37
proto-comics, 99–102

reading, direction of, 16, 76
Ryan, Marie-Laure, 42, 44

The Sandman, 32, 33, 34, 36, 38, 39,
    40–41, 42, 44, 45, 48, 53, 55, 118
Sense and Sensibility,
  by Jane Austen, 85–86, 88, 90
  Marvel Classics, 86, 87, 88, 89, 90
serialization, 38
Sinfest, 7–8, 12–13, 15–16, 47
Sir Henry Unton, 100–102
Shelley, Mary, 114–115
Shklovsky, Victor, 93
social knowledge, 10

space and time, 14–15, 34, 39, 75, 86, 91
speech bubbles, 8, 15, 24–25, 34, 39, 86, 100–101, 102, 103
speed line, 25
Sternberg, Meir, 35
story, 48, 49, 73–74, 80, 91, 99, 149
    and discourse, 34–36, 38, 39, 44, 80, 93, 128–129
    reliable, 48, 69
storytelling in comics, 2, 10, 32, 35
storyworld, 12, **19**, 22, 24, 45, 46, 65, 152
    embedded, 39
style, 55–56, 102
Superman, 74, 107, 109
superheroes, 56, 107, 109–111
surprise, 35–36
suspense, 34, 35–36, 47

terminology, 2, 8
time *see* space and time
transmedia storytelling, 73–74, 81
Todorov, Tzvetan, 36
Töpffer, Rodolphe, 15, 102–103
trade paperback, 84–85
trauma, 67, 134

Tristram Shandy by Laurence Sterne, 90–91, 93
    by Martin Rowson, 90–91, 92, 93

underground comics, **56–57**, 70, 117–118

V for Vendetta, 19, 20–21, 22, 25

Watchmen, 85, 107, 108, 109–110, 118–119, 123–124, 139
Ware, Chris, 55–56
web comics, 2, 4–6
Wertham, Fredric, 110–111, 112, 114
White, Hayden, 66
Williams, Raymond, 114
word-image relations, 7, 14, 23–24, 31–32, 34, 75, 79, 90, 99, 150
Wuthering Heights,
    by Emily Brontë, 74–75, 79–83
    Classics Illustrated, 75, 76–77, 79–81, 83
    Masterpiece, 75, 78, 79–81, 82, 83

The Yellow Kid, 103–104, 106, 115

Zunshine, Lisa, 86, 129